IDENTIFICATION OF SPECIFIC LEARNING DISABILITIES

E. LaMONTE OHLSON

117729

RESEARCH PRESS COMPANY
2612 NORTH MATTIS AVENUE
CHAMPAIGN, ILLINOIS 61820

*To my wife Rose,
and my children Blake, Sansanee, and Jason*

CONTENTS

FOREWORD

Perhaps more than any other area of exceptionality, learning disabilities is characterized by a great diversity of disciplines and theories relative to definition, identification, and instruction. Educators have traversed the extremes from refusing to recognize the existence of legitimate learning disorders to labeling children exhibiting only coordination problems or who fail to properly draw a diamond as being learning disabled. Parents have also displayed similar extremes when attempting to define learning disabilities.

Although volumes have been written on this subject, much of the literature is highly technical and biased toward the specific orientations of the respective authors, resulting in a contradictory and confusing information dais for the lay person. It is not uncommon to have a classroom teacher or school administrator state, "I still don't know what a learning disability is."

This book attempts to put the field of learning disabilities in proper perspective for such readers. The author begins by shedding light on the definition of learning disabilities. A chronological sequence of the various definitions is presented, providing the reader with insights into the historical development of the field. Although a general consensus is still nonexistent, of particular value is the author's identification of common traits found within the various definitions.

As much speculation exists regarding the causes of learning disabilities. No one factor can be singled out, and thus, the number of theories abounds. Etiological theories are effectively organized and synthesized in the second chapter, which permits the reader to gain a clear discernment of the causes of learning dysfunctions.

The major portion of this book, chapters 3–7, is devoted to the areas of screening and identification of learning disabilities. Initially considered are some of the issues relative to identification, such as the most efficacious age and method for screening. The fourth chapter deals with specific standardized instruments designed to assess cognitive, perceptual, and academic functioning. Attention is given not only to the individual test instruments but also to the process of standardized testing. The discussion of standardized measures is extended with the section on screening batteries, a relatively recent and unique approach to identifying learning disabled children. Less formal approaches to identification are provided in the next two chapters. Screening instruments which can be administered by individuals other than psychometrists are described in chapter 7. And the teacher's skill in identification through observation is assessed. The information provided on screening and identification may prove to be of tremendous value to persons assuming such responsibilities. In addition to being comprehensive, these chapters detail the parameters of the specific instruments/methods, assisting in determining their appropriateness for particular populations or administrators. Understandings are facilitated through the inclusion of tables listing the instruments and their respective attributes.

Finally, the book addresses the issue of how to teach learning disabled children. Major educational approaches are outlined with some attention given to the relative efficacy of the respective methods. The fact that this section provides an overview of the most representative and prevalent methodologies used in learning disabilities instruction contributes considerable merit to this book.

At a time when special education is having a tremendous impact on the entire realm of education, there is certainly a need for educators and other professionals to crystallize their understandings of the various exceptionalities, especially learning disabilities. This book is a valuable resource for both the novice as well as the more sophisticated individual who wishes to increase his/her skills in this area.

Department of Specialized Instruction   Dr. Gwen Cartledge
Cleveland State University
Cleveland, Ohio

PREFACE

The educational scene is currently being flooded with texts dealing with the identification and remediation (or diagnosis and treatment) of learning disorders. Analysis of the situation reveals the presence of many "experts" in the field who are writing about learning disorders as viewed from their own professional backgrounds. Educators write as though the problem is educational in nature and should be remediated within the present educational framework. Physicians state that the problem is physiological and must be dealt with in a biochemical manner. Optometrists argue the problem to be of a perceptual-motor-developmental nature needing treatment in some other specific manner. Psychologists view the problem from a learning standpoint. And the list goes on.

Inherent in any of these professions is a specific language or terminology which is germane only to that profession—jargon. It is jargon which facilitates communication within a profession while facilitating intercommunication between professions. Now, when the professions dealing with learning disabilities should be combining their efforts to attack the problem, they have allowed jargon to impede progress. There is no one answer descriptive of a learning disorder. Each child is an individual and therefore has individual problems. As a result, no one profession has the answer. Professional intercommunication and teamwork are essential to maximize efficient remediation or treatment.

Even though my profession is psychology, I have attempted to take a step toward encouraging interdisciplinary attention to the psycho-educational viewpoint by avoiding jargon as much as possible. Technical terms, of course, cannot be avoided. The descriptions of learning disabilities hopefully are concise and to the point. The tests included are currently used by professionals in varied fields, and criticism of tests and procedures is representative of current thinking. An additional aid is a list of latest editions of frequently used tests that are available commercially. The text is small enough to be used as a handbook by anyone, from professionals to parents dealing with the learning disabled. The author intends it to be a useful addition to any professional library and a valuable step toward an interdisciplinary philosophy of learning disabilities.

ACKNOWLEDGMENTS

As the completion of this book becomes a reality, the author finds words inadequate to express his feelings of indebtedness to his colleagues and family. Their patience, understanding, and encouragement throughout the entire time the manuscript was being prepared were major factors in the obtainment of the final goal.

More specifically, the author wishes to express his sincere appreciation to Dr. Gwen Cartledge, Cleveland State University, for her valuable assistance in the writing, organization, and formulation of chapter 8. Thanks to her major contribution, chapter 8 offers not only a review of teaching strategies but also includes new and pragmatic innovations and ideas in teaching learning disabled children.

Sincere indebtedness is also acknowledged to Mrs. Chloe Glasson, Cleveland Metropolitan General Hospital, whose criticism and revision of the chapter dealing with language development are of eminent significance.

Finally, the author wishes to express his appreciation to his wife, Rose, who even while completing her own doctorate, found time to continually review the manuscript for editorial and content concerns, as well as to support the author through the more difficult times.

CHAPTER 1 INTRODUCTION

HISTORICAL PERSPECTIVE

Seldom has a concept burst upon the educational scene with such a cataclysmic force as that of learning disorders. Although the early impetus of the unpublished work of Strauss and Lehtinen with the brain injured dates back from the late 1940's and early 1950's and the work of Orton in the area of dyslexia dates from the 1920's and the 1930's, the educational scene remained quite unaffected by this area as late as the early 1960's. McCarthy and McCarthy (1969) point out that with the possible exception of some isolated research practices in childhood aphasia and related language disturbances, activity in the area which is now called learning disability/disorder was largely sublimated or limited to sporadic attempts to develop new methods for remedial reading or new approaches to psychiatric or child guidance practice with children whose nonlearning was seen as a hostile response to parental rejection.

Universities, with rare exception, had no courses to train personnel in either diagnosis of a learning disability or teach-

1

ing the child who had one. The 1960 annual convention of the Council for Exceptional Children had not one program or paper which addressed itself to the topic under the various aliases (learning disabilities or disorders, among the multitudes) which have been used to describe the child who cannot learn. Then, a tremendous surge of work occurred in this area. At the 1965 annual convention for the Council for Exceptional Children the topic of learning disorders was second only to mental retardation in the number of sessions and papers presented.

Bateman (1966) specifies five factors which have been instrumental in bringing about newly crystallized interest in the child with a learning problem. (1) The increased growth of all other areas of special education has highlighted the problems of the "leftover" child with learning disorders. (2) The post-Sputnik period has put the emphasis on achievement, which focuses attention on many low achievers, especially those who have average or higher intelligence as do children with learning disorders. (3) The development of a broad educational movement toward a more scientific approach to all learning situations has occurred. This is an approach in which exact knowledge is sought of HOW each child learns and of the precise factors which influence his learning. (4) New diagnostic philosophies and instruments which have direct educational implications for curriculum have emerged. (5) There has been increased meaningful communication among educators, psychologists, and medical specialists, which has opened up significant research possibilities.

The child with learning problems has attracted the interest of general medicine, psychology, special education, neurology, psychiatry, optometry, pediatrics, ophthalmology, and education. Above all, this child's problems concern his teachers, parents, and himself.

Who is the child with a learning disability? From a historical perspective, "the full circle" has been traversed in an attempt to deal with this particular category of exceptionality (McCarthy and McCarthy, 1969). We have arrived once again at what Binet in 1909 described as "mental ortho-

2

pedics," the concept of educability of intelligence. The same attitude was apparent in the early work of Samuel Orton (1928) and Marion Monroe (1932). However, with the influence of the Freudian school of psychology, educators became involved in several decades of viewing problems as psychogenic manifestations of inner conflict. The "child who cannot learn" was seen as "the child who would not learn." After several decades of often fruitless efforts at manipulating the child's attitude toward learning, it became apparent to many psychiatrists, psychologists, and social workers that tender loving care or a deeper understanding of the child's own motivation could at best produce a child who was comfortable with his nonlearning.

Pioneer research at this point was begun in a variety of facilities, among them at Hawthorne Center where Rabinovitch (1964) found that the greatest number of emotionally disturbed children who recovered were among those who were tutored.

During the waning days of the psychodynamic approach to nonlearning, another thread of research and practice began to make an impact on the educational scene—the work of Alfred Strauss, Laura Lehtinen, and Newell Kephart and that of Rosa Hagin and Archie Selver with brain damaged children. The "brain damaged" era began slowly with the publishing of Strauss and Lehtinen's book (1947) and did not become full blown until the early 1960's. As a body of theory and research has developed over the past decade involving the child who does not learn, it seems apparent that strands from many disciplines are coalescing in the emergence of special learning disabilities as a significant educational concept (McCarthy and McCarthy, 1969).

EFFECTS OF DEFINITION

As both McCarthy and McCarthy (1969) and Barsch (1967) have pointed out, one of the most controversial issues in the field of special education is that of definition—the clear establishment of the identity of the child labeled "learning disabled." According to McCarthy and McCarthy (1969), the definition selected will dictate terminology to be used, prevalence figures, selection of criteria, characteristics of the population, and the choice of intervention strategies. Myklebust and Boshes (1969), in discussing prevalence, concluded that one could find as many learning disabled children as anticipated, providing one had a definition. Myklebust's implicit implication is that one's definition of learning disabilities determines how many learning disabled children are present. Ultimately, because what we *do* about a problem is more important than what we *call* it, definition must help specify at least the general parameters of appropriate educational intervention.

CONTROVERSY OVER SYNDROME
A number of child specialists (Gallagher, 1957; Birch, 1964; Werry, Weiss, and Douglas, 1964; Johnson and Myklebust, 1967; Kirk, 1968) voice doubt, some to a much greater extent than others, that the term "specific learning disability" or "minimal brain dysfunction" does in fact describe a syndrome. Though it is convenient to have a working label for these children, each of whom displays various psychological and behavioral characteristics, one view is that their great diversity is negative to the syndrome concept.

Dykman, Ackerman, Clements, and Peters (1971) consider further the idea of the specific learning dysfunction as a syndrome. A syndrome is a constellation of signs and symptoms that define an abnormality; for example, given X_1, X_2, . . . X_n, the probability of disease Y is substantial. This is not to say, however, that people with Y resemble one another in ways other than on the X's. Few argue that diabetes, to choose an arbitrary Y, is not a syndrome or that the cases diagnosed as diabetic are so heterogeneous that each should be treated individually rather than by principles established for all cases. Further, few people would argue that simply because people with diabetes fail to resemble one another in various personality or intellectual traits that the syndrome concept is unwarranted as applied to this disease.

By using a sufficient number of measures and tests, one

4

can define any syndrome out of existence, particularly by factor analytic studies. Perhaps, Dykman et al. point out, some of the writers adverse to the notion of a learning disability syndrome fall into such a trap. Although the learning disabled children are a diverse group, Dykman et al. conclude that they are sufficiently alike in certain basic underlying traits (the X's) to be subsumed under a "syndrome."

GENERIC VS. SPECIFIC TERM

Attempts to find or derive a precise, comprehensive definition of learning disorder are likely to be plagued with many difficulties due partly to problems related to both taxonomy and semantics. In a paper prepared for the Southern Regional Education Board and published in Hellmuth's book of readings, McDonald (1968, p. 1) reports the results of a questionnaire to which 35 educators and psychologists who work in the general area of learning disorders gave ". . . twenty-two terms which one or more of them used as exact synonyms for the title 'children with learning disabilities.' " The collection of terms reflects a wide range of orientations; for example: (1) educational—"remedial education," "educationally handicapped"; (2) medical—"brain injured," "minimal brain dysfunction"; and (3) psycholinguistic—"language disorders," "psycholinguistic disabilities."

McDonald (1968), in analyzing the results of his questionnaire, derives two basic categories around which definitions of learning disability seem to cluster. Some definers title "learning disorder" a generic term. The other group utilizes it to refer to a specific subgroup of children.

The group which considers learning disability as a generic term refers to all children who have difficulty in acquiring the skills, concepts, and competencies appropriate to their age potential as learning disabled. The key word to most of these definers is "underachievement." They see children with learning disorders as those who have a marked discrepancy between a measure of personal potential and present performance. An example of this view is: Learning disability cannot be viewed as a distinct clinical entity in itself, but must be

5

approached as a symptom reflecting disorder in one or more of the many processes involved in academic learning. Principal among these processes are general intelligence, specific capacities, developmental readiness, emotional freedom to learn, motivation, and opportunity (Rabinovitch, 1959).

The second group of respondents to McDonald's questionnaire (those who consider "learning disability as a discrete group") maintain that the learning disability population can be clearly and operationally defined. A representative statement of this view is that a mere generic concept is nonsensical, and an operational definition is required by every investigation in order to specify how the term is being used.

The dichotomy between a generic vs. a discrete perspective as a definition of learning disability is just one of the numerous discrepancies which must be contended with in attempting to solidify a view of the nature of learning disabilities.

DIVERGENCE OF TERMINOLOGY
USED BY AUTHORITATIVE BODIES

Bateman (1966) strengthens McDonald's findings concerning the diversity of some of the vast differences in learning disability language by pointing to developmental differences among bodies and organizations that should, by reason of their positions, be considered authorities. The U.S. Office of Education includes children with learning problems in the category of orthopedically handicapped and health-impaired children. California uses the term "educationally handicapped" and includes within it the two categories of emotionally disturbed and neurologically impaired. In contrast, Michigan requires that children admitted to its programs be "perceptually handicapped" and be totally free from emotional or psychiatric problems (Rabinovitch, 1964). Illinois recognizes children with learning disorders as a subcategory of "maladjusted" children. Separate provisions thus apply to children with emotional problems and to those with social problems associated with cultural deprivation or educational retardation. The divergence of terminology suggested by

6

these four examples can be increased by almost the total number of state programs, private schools, clinics, and individual therapists dealing with these children. The entangled web of terminology makes meaningful communication between institutions and individuals difficult.

SOME PREVALENT DEFINITIONS

Five Definitions Accepted by the Majority

No current definition of "learning disability" is acceptable to all professionals concerned with the area. It is very unlikely that any one definition could find total acceptance in the foreseeable future (Ferrald and Schamber, 1973). McCarthy and McCarthy (1969), however, suggest that there are six or seven prevalent definitions which seem acceptable to a majority of the practitioners in the field. Among these are the definitions of Task Force I [later referred to as Phase I (Clements, 1966)], Task Force II [later referred to as Phase II (Haring and Bateman, 1969)], The Association for Children with Learning Disabilities (1967), The Council for Exceptional Children (1967), and a recent definition of Dr. Samuel Kirk (1967). Perhaps examination of these will reveal significant parallels and points of agreement, thereby aiding in the attempt to clarify further just what a learning disability is.

Association for Children with Learning Disabilities (1967) A child with learning disabilities is one with adequate mental ability, sensory processes, and emotional stability who has a limited number of specific deficits in perceptual, integrative, or expressive processes which severely impair learning efficiency. This includes children who have central nervous system dysfunction which is expressed primarily in impaired learning efficiency.

Council for Exceptional Children (CEC) (1967) According to CEC, children with special learning disabilities are those who exhibit a disorder in one or more of the basic psychological

7

processes involved in understanding or in using verbal or written language. These may be manifested in problems of listening, thinking, talking, reading, writing, spelling, or doing arithmetic. They include conditions which have been referred to as perceptual handicaps, brain injury, minimal brain dysfunction, dyslexia, developmental aphasia, etc. They do not include learning problems which are due primarily to visual, hearing, or motor handicaps, to mental retardation, emotional disturbance, or to environmental disadvantage.

HEW—Phase I (Clements, 1966) The diagnostic categories subsumed under the rubric of minimal brain dysfunction refer to those children who are of average or above general intelligence with learning and/or behavior difficulties ranging from mild to most severe. The difficulties are due to subtle deviations arising from genetic variations, biochemical irregularities, perinatal brain insults, and/or illnesses and injuries sustained during the years critical for the development and maturation of those parts of the central nervous system having to do with perception, language, inhibition of impulses, and motor control.

HEW—Phase II (Haring and Bateman, 1969) Children with learning disabilities are those (1) who manifest an educationally significant discrepancy between estimated academic potential and actual level of academic functioning as related to dysfunctioning in the learning process; (2) who may or may not show demonstrable deviation in central nervous system functioning; and (3) whose disabilities are secondary to central mental retardation, cultural, sensory and/or educational deprivation, or environmentally produced serious emotional disturbance. (This was one of two definitions offered.)

Kirk, S. A. (1967) A learning disability refers to a specific retardation or disorder in one or more of the processes of speech, language, perception, behavior, reading, spelling, writing, or arithmetic, resulting from a possible cerebral dysfunction and/or emotional or behavioral disturbance and not

8

from mental retardation, sensory deprivation, or cultural or instructional factors.

Similarities in these Definitions Of these five current definitions which seem acceptable to the majority of practitioners in the field, all have two concepts in common: the first is the *intact clause*. Definers seem to agree that the child with the learning disability is basically an intact organism. There is general agreement that the learning disability is *not* primarily due to visual, hearing, or motor handicaps, to mental retardation, emotional disturbance, or to the environmental disadvantages.

The second concept which appears across these definitions is the *discrepancy clause*. Oftentimes, authors refer to the discrepancy phenomena in various ways. For example, Rappaport (1966) has referred to "insufficiencies," Gallagher (1966) to "imbalances," and Ashlock and Stephen (1966) to "gaps." These definitions seem to adhere to this principle of disparity. What the concept implies is that the learning disabled child can be recognized by the presence of a meaningful difference between what he is capable of doing and what he is actually accomplishing; that is, a marked underachievement in school-related activities.

In determining an educationally significant discrepancy, there are no rigid, all-encompassing rules or formulas to follow. Observation of lagging academic performance can be quantified through use of suitable standardized achievement tests. To satisfy the definition of learning disorder, a child's observed achievement level must be unexpectedly low when compared with his mental ability and other factors.

A third area of similarity among most of these definitions is the hypothesis that specific learning disabilities are observable symptoms of underlying neurologic disorganization (Clements, 1966). Most researchers agree that a variety of central nervous system impairments appear to be associated with specific learning disability and have noted that groups of learning disabled children present an unusually high incidence of positive neurological signs. But the degree to which these signs are manifestations of, or merely associated with, learning disability has yet to be fully demonstrated.

However, many pupils who demonstrate one or another of the learning disorders, such as dyslexia, dysphasia, and dysgraphia, have undergone neurological evaluations with results that do not support the suppositions of central nervous system impairment. Whether due to the subtle nature of the hypothesized organic deviations or due to the weakness of present-day medical diagnostic techniques, lack of positive neurological evidence is not an uncommon occurrence among children who manifest learning disorders.

Several of the foregoing definitions are characterized by an *exclusion clause* which attempts to define the learning disability in terms of those categories of children already excluded. Unlike other types of exceptional children, the learning disabled child is often defined in terms of things he does NOT possess. Supposedly, children without adequate intellectual ability are already excluded from the mainstream of education under the categorical label "mental retardation," while children with emotional problems have already been excluded and placed in special classes for the "emotionally disturbed." Similarly, children with a sensory deficit or who have been educationally or culturally deprived are excluded. The decision not to include these other exceptional children among the learning disabled is arbitrary. Certainly there are mentally retarded children who can satisfy all the provisions of the definition of specific learning disability, but because their learning difficulties are secondary to the more serious handicap or subnormality, they are placed in programs for the mentally retarded.

A More Recent Definition

One of the most recent definitions of learning disability to achieve acclaim has been advanced by the Council for Exceptional Children (1971): A child with learning disabilities is one with adequate mental ability (i.e., intelligence), sensory process, and emotional stability but evidences specific deficits in perceptual, integrative, or expressive processes. The outcome is, therefore, a child who suffers from severely impaired learning efficiency.

Denhoff, Hainsworth, and Hainsworth (1971) see this definition as changing the focus from deficits in learning products to inefficiencies in processes. Instead of looking for the failure of academic learning, the educator is directed to become aware of inadequate processing skills. This opens the way for early identification and help for the child with learning disabilities.

If any trend in recent definitions could be isolated, it would be one toward a definition that is educationally relevant—one which offers a remediation strategy. The 1971 definition by the Council for Exceptional Children is in this vein.

EFFECTS ON PREVALENCE
The prevalence of children with learning disorders is a direct function of definition and identification procedures. The task in isolating incidences of learning disabilities is doubly difficult since no single objective measure can be used. Bruininks (1971), in a survey of research findings by leading authorities on prevalence estimates of children with severe learning difficulties, found somewhat of a consistency, with figures ranging mostly from 10 percent to 15 percent of the school population. The studies reviewed consisted of varying sample specifications, and defining criteria differed.

Problems With Applying Achievement Formulas
There are problems with each method of estimation. Obviously, figures from authorities lack any great degree of validity due to the diversity of predictions. Likewise, the application of achievement formulas to school populations has some drawbacks. Findings suggest (Neville and Bruininks, 1972) that applying achievement expectancy formulas to school populations increases the likelihood of identifying as poor achievers many children who actually represent errors in measurement. A long standing research axiom is that persons scoring high or low on one measure will likely yield less extreme scores by chance along another measure. Neville and

11

Bruininks (1972) suggest that the use of mental age capital-izes on statistical regression, thereby identifying as learning disabled an unknown number of children who merely exem-plify measurement errors.

Bateman (1966) points out several drawbacks with using an achievement deficit as a criterion for a learning disorder. First, there are a number of problems in determining ex-pected achievement levels. Second, many educators do not wish to include in the learning disabled category the child whose poor achievement is related to motivational, instruc-tional, cultural, or sensory difficulties. A third problem is that school achievement is relative to geographic, cultural, and economic factors. Finally, some children with severe visuo-motor problems would be excluded if school achieve-ment were the sole criterion.

McGrady (1970) brings out further difficulty with using underachievement as a definer of learning disability. If the practice of taking the lowest 10 percent or 5 percent of the school-age children and labeling them as learning disabled is continued, there will continue to be a certain percentage of learning disabled forever—regardless of what strategies are used. McGrady recommends defining learning and its disabili-ties according to competencies and skills, not age levels, nor grade levels, nor percentiles. Only when this is done, he be-lieves, the incidence statistics will truly mean something.

Ullman (1969) points out that assuming a certain degree of underachievement as being a criterion for learning dis-ability leads to an artificial increase in prevalence of learning disabled *with age.* A similar critic with the fixed differences approach for varying grade levels also assumes that incre-ments are constant in academic growth across grade levels. This assumption has no basis since growth of academic skills with age typically assumes the shape of a negatively accelerat-ing curve rather than that of a linear curve (Simmons and Shapiro, 1968).

SUMMARY
The concept of learning disorders is a fairly recent one. Be-

12

cause the "cause and cure" of a learning disorder is so nebulous, many disciplines other than education have entered the field of learning disabilities; namely, general medicine, psychology, special education, neurology, psychiatry, optometry, pediatrics, and ophthalmology.

Since this field is so new, the definition of a learning disability has been much in debate. Many researchers have proposed definitions for learning disability depending upon their own special interests. In the early era of research in this area, a child of normal intelligence who had difficulty learning was thought to have some brain damage or dysfunction. Later some decided learning disability was part of an overall syndrome. All types of speculations about etiology and definitions have ensued. As a result, the entangled web of terminology makes meaningful communication between institutions and individuals difficult.

Most definitions of learning disability state the child is intact, but that some discrepancy exists, usually in the educational performance area. Another area of similarity of these definitions is that a learning disability is an observable result of some underlying cause.

There is some disagreement about the prevalence of learning disability; however, it is a direct function of definition, identification procedures, and presumed etiology. As can be readily seen, identifying the children with learning problems and determining why they have them will be in doubt for some time to come.

CHAPTER 2   THE ETIOLOGY OF
LEARNING DISABILITIES

Theories of the etiology of learning disorders have not missed many bases. The postulated sites of the underlying causes of learning problems range from the brain, to the psyche, the genes, the biochemical system, the eyes and ears, and even the "whole" child (Bateman, 1966). Reviews of the extensive literature on the etiology of learning problems include those by Money (1962); Kass (1963); de Hirsch, Jansky, and Langford (1965); and Whitsell (1965).

PERSPECTIVE OF MYERS AND HAMMILL

One rather well-formulated perspective of the etiology of learning disabilities is proposed by Myers and Hammill (1969). They use the term "specific learning disability" and define it as a symptom of internal conditions within the child, such as suboptimal neurological functioning or inadequate programming of essentially normal nervous tissue. Myers and Hammill (1969) maintain that behavioral manifestations or characteristics of learning disabled children are much the same regardless of etiology.

15

Thus in this chapter, major consideration is given to two broad etiological categories noted by Myers and Hammill—(1) organically based etiologies and (2) environmentally based etiologies. Exemplifying the organically based category are neurological malfunctions involving such organic deviations as genetic variations, biochemical irregularities, and brain insults (injuries or damages), all of which may cause the brain to function abnormally. Examples of environmentally based deficits include experiences which inhibit the development of percepts underlying one or more basic skills.

Organically Based Etiologies

Minimal Brain Dysfunction Under the organically based etiologies falls the concept of minimal brain dysfunction. Many researchers and clinicians in the field maintain that specific learning disabilities are caused primarily by malfunction of the central nervous system. Since this system operates as a processor of information, inferior performance in any of its processes can seriously inhibit or retard the child's ability to learn or respond (Griffiths and Griffiths, 1974).

Myers and Hammill (1969) illustrate their conception of the relationship between brain dysfunction and learning disorders as two overlapping circles (see Figure 1).

Circle A represents children with medically diagnosed brain dysfunction. Circle B depicts children with demonstrable, educationally defined learning disorders. Learning disordered cases arising primarily from and in association with brain dysfunction are included in the shaded area common to both circles. Since the incidence of learning disability among children with or without brain dysfunction is not clearly established, the circles and their overlap area are not, and cannot, be drawn to scale.

A child could be placed in one of the following categories:
1. Symptoms of brain dysfunction but no detectable learning disability
2. Both brain dysfunction and learning disability

16

*Figure 1. Relationship between Brain Dysfunction and
Learning Disorders.*

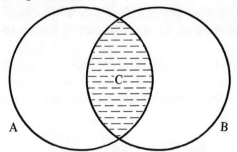

A—Medically diagnosed brain dysfunction
B—Demonstrable, educationally defined learning disorders
C—Learning disorders not clearly defined medically or educationally
    but a combination of both

From *Methods for learning disorders* by P. I. Myers and D. D. Hammill.
New York: John Wiley and Sons, 1969. Used with permission.

3. Evidence of learning disability but no observable sign of
brain malfunction

The electroencephalogram has been the instrument used
most widely by physicians in the identification process for
neurological impairment. Research findings which attempt to
correlate EEG ratings with psychological test functions of
learning disability are abundant. Conclusions from these
studies range from high correlations to little or no relationship. Freeman (1967) maintains that the EEG appears to be
regarded with more awe than it deserves. He points to many
technical problems in its use. He feels the mystique about the
instrument must be dispelled. Freeman attributes the influ-
ences of the EEG among educators to the inundation of the
literature with poorly done papers describing children with
supposed minimal brain damage.

McGrady (1970) found that a major problem with EEG
was subjectivity of the readings. When two readers on two
separate sets of EEG's were compared, findings showed they
agreed sometimes only 70 percent, sometimes 60 percent of
the time. Further findings by McGrady (1970) revealed that
even 29 percent of children *without* learning disabilities in

17

this sample showed EEG abnormalities. According to McGrady, all that may be concluded when examining the EEG reading of any child, therefore, is that there is a higher probability of getting an abnormality if the child has a learning disability.

Freeman (1967), in a more positive perspective, concludes that the EEG does have value when used in conjunction with a multifaceted evaluation and full recognition of its limitations.

Environmentally Based Etiologies

As noted earlier, Myers and Hammill (1969) consider environmental causes of learning disorders in addition to the category of organically based etiologies. They subdivide the environmental domain into (a) insufficient early perceptual motor experience and (b) emotional maladjustment.

Insufficient Early Perceptual Motor Experience Insufficient perceptual motor experience is demonstrated by studies which have used animals as subjects. Results suggest that mode of rearing has a permanent effect on behavior at maturity, particularly intelligent behavior (Hebb, 1958). An example is afforded by Frantz (1965), who studied the effects of visual experience on perceptual development.

Potentially harmful psychological experiments must necessarily use animals as subjects; generalization of these results to humans and subsequent conclusions are made with understandable caution. Speaking about children, Frantz has suggested:

Perception precedes action and early perceptual experience is necessary for the development of coordinated and visually directed behavior. The perfection of sensorimotor coordination will in turn increase the efficiency of perceptual progress (1966, p. 144).

Frantz's remarks seem in basic agreement with those of Kephart (1960), who comments at length regarding "a modern dilemma" facing today's children. Although present civili-

18

zation requires the perfection of sensorimotor processes, the *practice* opportunity necessary for children to develop the processes adequately is decreased, thus perceptual development is hindered.

Emotional Maladjustment The second division of environmental etiologies discussed by Myers and Hammill is that of the effect of emotional disturbances. Cited as references are Gellhorn and Loofborrow (1963), who suggest that emotional reactions, even if they are not overt, play an important part in perception. The validity of their statement is supported in part by (1) the work of Frostig, Lefever, and Whittlesey (1963), who in a study of preschool and primary-grade children related disabilities in visual perception to problems in learning and behavior, and (2) the findings of Chansky (1958), Boise (1955), Berkowitz and Rothman (1955), and Tamkin (1960), which report significant correlation between emotional disturbances and reading retardation.

In a more recent consideration of the social and emotional factors surrounding learning disorders, Connolly (1971) has concluded that despite numerous statements concerning the issue, relatively few writers have attempted to validate their opinions. Furthermore, of those who have sought to provide hard research data to verify their beliefs, many have obtained primarily nonsignificant findings when comparing personality variables of an experimental group of learning disability subjects with a control group of normals (Connolly, 1969; Myklebust and Boshes, 1969; and Goldstein, 1970). The conclusion by Connolly is that although a majority of writers in the field seems to believe that learning disorders and emotional problems are related, there is a paucity of research evidence to substantiate this belief.

PERSPECTIVE OF BATEMAN
Bateman (1966) examines the etiology of learning disabilities in terms of four different classifications from Myers and Hammill: (1) cerebral dominance, (2) brain damage or dysfunction, (3) maturational lag, and (4) multifactor theories.

19

Cerebral Dominance

The role of *cerebral dominance* in learning problems has been discussed since Orton (1928) postulated faulty cerebral dominance as a factor in developmental dyslexia. He also emphasized the relation of dyslexia to other developmental language disorders such as congenital word deafness, motor speech delay, and stuttering, as well as developmental apraxia.

Zangwill (1960) reviewed the question of cerebral dominance in dyslexia and concluded that a typical or mixed dominance is a characteristic of a large number of backward readers. Brain (1961) summarized the present concept of the importance of an abnormality of cerebral dominance in dyslexia, stating, "It is probable that in such cases the failure to establish a dominant hemisphere is the *result* and not the cause of congenital abnormalities of brain function which also express themselves in disabilities of speech, reading, and writing" (p. 138).

Brain Damage

Brain damage as described by Bateman is very similar to the description by Myers and Hammill (1969). Bateman adds to the discussion specific areas of the brain which have been implicated in etiological theory: the angular gyrus (Hinshelwood, 1917); the parietal lobes and the parietal-occipital lobes (Rabinovitch, 1959); the second frontal gyrus (Wernicke in 1874, as reported by Penfield and Roberts, 1959); and the connection between the cortical speech mechanism and the brain stem centrecephalic system (Penfield and Roberts, 1959).

Maturational Lag

Bateman refers to the work of Bender (1958) in developing the concept of *maturational lag.* Bender's basic postulate is that those parts of the neopallium which serve the functions of unilateral dominance, handedness, eyedness, visual and auditory symbol recognition, and language (spoken and written) show a wider range of maturation age than do other

20

parts.

According to Bender, the syndrome resulting from this maturational lag includes some of the following characteristics: slower maturation of language skills, especially reading; slower maturation in neurological signs and awkwardness, and uneven intellectual development; subsequent reading disability; poorly established cortical dominance; right-left confusion; immature personality; a far greater frequency in boys than girls; and familial history indicating a lag in maturation of cortical dominance.

Bender considers that the concept of maturational lag refers to functional areas of the brain and personality and to a slow differentiation of pattern; it does not imply a structural deficiency, loss, or necessarily even a limitation of potential.

Multifactor Approach
The fourth classification which Bateman considers is the *multifactor* approach to the etiology of learning problems. Emphasis in this category is on environmental, instructional, emotional, and motivational factors not included in single-factor theories. According to Bateman, the children considered in the multifactor theories (Monroe, 1932; Rabinovitch and Ingram, 1962; and Robinson, 1946) often have less severe disabilities than do those discussed by the advocates of single-factor etiologies.

Hammill and Bartel (1975), as well as Bateman, present multifactor approaches to explain the etiology of learning disabilities.

SOME SINGLE-FACTOR ETIOLOGIES
The following are a number of researchers who, in contrast, have focused on *one* specific factor as being all-important.

Deficiencies in Attention
Dykman, Ackerman, Clements, and Peters (1971) link organically based deficiencies in attention with poorer performance, slower reaction time, and the decreased physiological

reactivity of learning disabled children in learning situations. They cite two pieces of indirect evidence: (1) Neurophysiological research has revealed many of the brain mechanisms involved in attention and alertness, and (2) these mechanisms are critical in mediating. These *autonomic* and *somatic* responses have been found to separate learning disability cases and controls.

Hyperactive learning disabled children appear to be overattentive to their environment, whereas hypoactive ones are underattentive. The net effect of over- or under-attention on performance is the same (Luria, 1961). Hyperactives tend to switch in too many familiar stimuli. Dykman et al. (1971) believe that in all learning disabled children there is considerable inertia in moving from the open to the closed state, or the reverse, and even from one action to another. This critical difference has often been emphasized as the mobility of the nervous process.

There is much research evidence, according to Dykman et al., to support the viewpoint of defective attention as central to learning disabilities. No piece of this evidence alone is very convincing, but collectively it is very impressive. Such research includes the work of Strauss and Lehtinen, 1947; Myklebust, 1954; Luria, 1961; Zeaman and House, 1963; Trabasso, 1968; and Senf and Freundl, 1971.

Disorders in Genes

Another base for the underlying cause of learning disorders is the genes. In a recent study (Silver, 1971) of 556 individuals with the neurological learning disability syndrome, data were collected on prenatal and perinatal difficulties, medical problems, and family history of similar learning difficulties. In the total study, 29.6 percent of the children had a positive family history of similar learning disorders. That part of the data which was most complete and accurate yielded a 39.4 percent figure for children who had a positive family history. Even though there was a history of prenatal, perinatal, or postnatal difficulties in some children, siblings without a history of such difficulties also had learning disabilities. Silver concluded that the etiologic factor with some of the children having this syndrome is an inherited central nervous system dysfunction rather than brain damage.

Hermann (1956, 1959) also presented convincing evidence for a hereditary form of dyslexia with a fundamental disturbance. He reported that dyslexic children often show right/left disorientation, mixed laterality, and finger agnosia. Hermann pointed out that all pairs of uniovular twins reported up to 1959 showed concordance in word blindness. He concluded that heredity is a decisive factor in the occurrence of constitutional dyslexia, whereas environmental factors are of minor importance.

Endocrine System and Chromosomal Makeup
Grenn and Perlman (1971) focus on the endocrine system and chromosome makeup in the etiology of learning disorders. They maintain that sections of the endocrine system are essential to normal brain development, maturation, and intellectual function. Their research indicates that gross deficiencies of thyroid hormone secretions, disturbances in blood sugar levels, and abnormal chromosomal inheritance can cause permanent alterations in behavior and intellectual function. They found alterations in chromosomal constitution within a population of children attending a learning disability clinic. Finally, they posit that minor alterations of blood sugar, calcium, and thyroid hormone may cause specific learning problems in children, but considerably more research is needed.

Malnutrition
Birch and Grotberg (1971) consider malnutrition as a possible factor which is very likely related to learning problems. Their survey of malnutrition research indicates nutritional factors at a number of different levels contribute significantly to depressed intellectual development and learning failure. These effects may be produced (1) directly as the consequences of irreparable alterations of the nervous system or (2) indirectly as a result of ways in which the learning experience of the developing organism may be significantly interfered

23

with at a critical point in the developmental course.

Interaction
A totally different approach to the etiology of learning disabilities is assumed by Adelman (1970), who looks at the causes of learning disabilities from an interaction viewpoint. According to this approach, the child's success in the classroom seems dependent upon the congruity of his characteristics with the characteristics of the classroom in which he is required to perform.

It is hypothesized that the greater the congruity between a youngster's characteristics and the characteristics of the program in which he is required to perform, the greater the likelihood of school success; conversely, the greater the discrepancy between the child's characteristics and the program's characteristics, the greater the likelihood of poor school performance. Following from this reasoning, it is further hypothesized that the teacher's achieving personalized instruction leads to fewer children in the classroom who exhibit learning problems.

SUMMARY
Theories of the etiology of learning disability are many and varied. Myers and Hammill (1969) identify two types: organic and environmental. Organic etiologies are the result of some organic malfunction or injury or biochemical imbalance. Environmental etiologies include insufficient perceptual motor experience and emotional maladjustment. Bateman (1966) outlines four other classifications of etiology: cerebral dominance; brain damage or dysfunction; maturational lag; and multifactor theories. Silver (1971) and Hermann (1956) include genetics as an etiology. There is a possibility that disturbances of the endocrine system may have an effect.

Thus, as was originally stated, researchers do come at the etiology of learning disabilities from a variety of directions. Some of the etiological factors presented here would be perhaps classified as more primary than others. For example, malnutrition might very well be the cause of malfunction of the central nervous system, which more directly results in a learning disability. Suffice it to say that coverage has been given to a large portion of the causes of learning disabilities which appear in the literature.

Whatever is causing the learning problem, nothing can be done until the child's exceptionality is discovered. For this reason identification techniques are of the utmost importance.

CHAPTER 3 THE IDENTIFICATION OF LEARNING DISABILITIES

"Efficient and effective techniques must be found to identify learning disabilities among large populations of school children" (Bryan and McGrady, 1972, p. 199). Two assumptions underlie this statement, according to Bryan and McGrady: (1) Among all the children who fail to learn in school, varying degrees and types of deficits are associated with a variety of conditions. (2) If any type of learning disability is to be understood, a thorough assessment must be made. Such an evaluation must be individualized; however, individualized clinical or psycho-educational assessment is time consuming and expensive. Considerable history taking, testing, consultation, and staffing must occur and must be coordinated. It is impossible to assume that many children can be served through such procedures. Methods that screen large populations of children are being devised so the least number of children necessary will be submitted to the entire diagnostic process. A growing number of primary schools are incorporating some type of screening into their regular program (Slingerland, 1966).

SCOPE OF EARLY IDENTIFICATION

Although in recent years the need for prompt diagnosis of children with learning disabilities has been emphasized so treatment and training may be initiated to enhance the remediation of learning deficits, some disagreement ensues over specifics: Which approach is best, the group screening instrument or the individually administered screen? How early is too early, or is it ever too early for identification of a learning disability? Are teacher-completed behavior rating scales as informative a screen as the more traditional, standardized tests?

Value of Early Identification

A considerable body of research, amassing since 1960, has been advocating the early identification of learning disabilities. Haring and Ridgway (1967) point to the almost certain failure of the learning disabled child in the conventional school program. Often the child must suffer months and sometimes years of unsuccessful work before he receives remedial aid. Invariably this failure leads to compounded and more serious problems when the school program demands of the child use of skills that he has never developed.

To prevent serious learning problems from occurring, identification of the child should be as early as possible according to Haring and Ridgway. Early identification of problems permits better use of the critical learning periods. Given this information, the teacher is able to construct an appropriate instructional program that will develop the child's skills, experience, and potential, while preventing or relieving some of the problems arising from past failure.

Rogolsky (1968-1969) maintains (if large numbers of children are to be helped effectively) early identification is necessary. Comprehensive screening detecting a wide variety of handicaps is needed so that all children who might benefit from an individualized or special program will be recognized. Kindergarten screening that isolates learning disability cases facilitates placement of children. It offers the teacher an objective aid when she considers the child's advancement or retention or the grouping of children within the classroom. Screening will allow the school to forego rigid adherence to chronological age as a basis of grade placement.

Disadvantages of Early Identification

As the foregoing references indicate, there is overwhelming support for early identification of learning problems. Keogh and Becker (1973), however, in a very thorough analysis of early identification, have formulated the following pertinent questions on the subject.

The whole concept of early identification comes from the physical disability or disease model, they point out, an approach based on several assumptions: (1) The condition to be identified is already existent in the child. (2) The diagnosis carries a specified direction or prescription for treament. (3) The sooner treatment begins, the greater the likelihood of its impact. Treatment may prevent development of other deleterious conditions, or it may minimize compounding problems. Nevertheless, when we seek to identify preschool or kindergarten children who we fear may become learning failures, we are, in fact, hypothesizing rather than confirming. Oftentimes the conditions have not yet developed or are only in very preliminary stages.

Keogh and Becker further point to a paradox which exists in the research on early identification. If early identification and diagnosis are insightful and remedial implementation successful, the preschool or kindergarten high-risk child would receive the kind of attention and help that results in successful school performance. In essence, he would no longer be high risk and would instead be a successful achiever. Predictive validity of the identification instruments would, therefore, be low. In such a case, success with the child would negate accuracy of prediction. Research on development of predictive tools is limited by ethical considerations. Having identified a child as high risk, the researcher is obligated to interfere, thus limiting examination of the long-term predictive validity of the instruments.

Keogh and Becker conclude that the benefits of early

identification of learning disabilities is advantageous if the process leads to prevention, early treatment, or constructive counseling. However, the authors go on to say that there are deficits to early identification when the identification process is a mere academic exercise which can be potentially harmful to the child and his family.

Faust (1970) issues another warning. In a review of cognitive and language factors in early identification, he emphasizes that individual characteristics change as a function of interaction with the environment and that there are few "inherent, stable traits of the individual" (p. 346) that allow long-term prediction. Reading and other school learning tasks consist of many components and require perceptual, cognitive, and motor skills because child characteristics vary in relation to the learning task and situation. Thus, many facets of the child's development and experience may be directly relevant to tasks to be learned. Few clear one-to-one relationships exist between specific preschool characteristics and specific school learnings. Therefore, care must be taken in attempting to predict who will succeed and who will have difficulty in learning.

The term self-fulfilling prophecy, used by Rosenthal and Jacobson (1966) to describe effects of teacher expectancy on pupil performance, may be applicable to the early identification issue. Although that study has been criticized (Thorndike, 1968; Snow, 1969), the effect must be reckoned with. When children are identified as high risk, a set of expectancies, anxieties, and differential treatment patterns may develop. Effects may be particularly insidious because preschool or kindergarten children have not yet developed the deficit conditions for which they were identified. The act of predicting may have a built-in expectancy phenomenon. Because effects of parent and teacher anxieties upon a child are uncertain and the possibility that the effect of an expectancy involved in prediction may be harmful, the ethical issues relating to programs of early identification deserve consideration.

CONTROVERSY OVER SCREENING INSTRUMENTS

Group vs. Individual Screening

A second subject of contention is the most advantageous type of screening instrument—group vs. individual. Buktenica (1971), an advocate of the group screening instrument, lists the three functions of the ideal screening instrument as (1) prediction of children who are high risk, (2) description of each child's learning problem, and (3) production of information necessary for programs aimed at prevention of learning disabilities.

Buktenica views the group screening situations as having the potential to effect more congruence between learners and the task. Because group instruments are given in the criterion setting—the classroom, not a laboratory—the characteristics of a learner are assessed in a situation analogous to one where he will be expected to learn. Adequate group screening decreases the need for individual diagnostic procedures which are inappropriate for use with large numbers of children. Prediction of academic success with individually administered tests has not been demonstrated to be more accurate than with group tests, and economy of effort is considerably more for group screening procedures. Considering these factors, Buktenica maintains that perhaps group screening procedures rather than individual diagnostics should be used for detecting learning disabilities.

There are, however, disadvantages to the group approach. The tendency has been to use group academic achievement tests as the major screen. This fails for several reasons (Bryan and McGrady, 1972): (1) Learning disability becomes synonymous with low achievement relative to potential. The learning disabled child merely becomes the child who falls in the lowest 5 to 10 percent, depending on the arbitrary cutoff points established by the screeners. (2) Most group screening tests used in the schools include only academic areas and arithmetic. In addition, the tests never consider behavioral problems which may interact with academic-learning performance. (3) Many important intellectual cognitive, perceptual, and language functions cannot be measured by group tests. Abilities such as sequencing of information, memory of items when presented by various modes, and oral expression need individual assessment.

Further problems faced in the group screening situation that do not exist in the individual test are the greater possibility of individual children being disturbed by other children or the possibility that children taking the group test are working at a rate or in a manner contingent upon what others are doing rather than what they would do individually. Further, there is less control over administration of group tests such as in the giving of instructions, adhering to time limits when appropriate, lack of suitable test supervision plus a host of other intervening test variables. As a result of the greater variability of administration procedures, standardization of the test is affected and therefore test results are biased.

Teacher Rating Scales
Another kind of alternative relatively new to the educational scene is the teacher rating scale. Using this type of instrument, the classroom teacher at her convenience evaluates the various behaviors of one or all students in a checklist-type format. The teacher's rating scale reflects accurately and comprehensively a child's classroom behavior. Disadvantages of this type of instrument include its subjectiveness, the halo effect often found around exceptional children, and sometimes ill-defined domains of behavior which the teacher must attempt to rate.

INSTRUMENTS COVERED IN THIS BOOK
The search for the "best" variety of instrument goes on. Consideration will now be given to some of the instruments that have actually been used in the identification of learning disabilities. The first category to be examined will be standardized tests—those instruments that the psychologist has traditionally utilized in his diagnostic work-up (chapter 4).

Next will be a look at some of the more recent learning

disability screening batteries which are often composed of portions of complete forms of several standardized tests—specifically those tests that most efficiently assess specific conditions under investigation (chapter 5).

Following this, consideration will be given to specific instruments which have been developed—mostly in the last 10 years—for screening high-risk learning problem children (chapter 6). Some of these are teacher-administered; others are given by psychologists or other specialists. Both group and individual tests are represented in this category.

Finally, the behavior rating scale as a screening instrument will be evaluated (chapter 7). The teacher plays the dominant role in identifying learning problem candidates.

Interwoven in the discussion of each of these varieties of diagnostic/screening devices will be an analysis of the benefits and deficits of each category.

SUMMARY

In an endeavor to identify learning disabled children, one must confront some of the following problems: Which type of instrument is best, the group test or the individual test? How early can the testing be done and still provide valid measurements? And, are behavior rating scales as informative as the more traditional standardized tests?

Most educators agree, the earlier the learning disabled child is identified, the better. This type of thinking makes several assumptions: (1) The condition already exists in the child. (2) A diagnosis carries a prescription for treatment. (3) The sooner treatment begins, the greater will be the impact of the treatment. A paradox also exists. If early remedial treatment is successful, the child will not be an under-achiever. This, therefore, reduces the predictive validity of the instrument.

When dealing with early identification, teachers must take care that pupil performance does not follow the "self-fulfilling prophecy." The act of predicting may have a built-in expectancy phenomenon.

The advantages and disadvantages of the screening instrument must be weighed with regard to the variables at hand. Group tests are economical, but specific variables are difficult to control. Individual tests are more time consuming but oftentimes produce more specific diagnostic information. The following chapters will discuss some of the more common group and individual screening instruments and outline their advantages and disadvantages as well as other aspects of their application.

CHAPTER 4   DETECTION THROUGH FORMAL STANDARDIZED TESTS

General principles of diagnostic procedures for learning disabilities are presented by Gallagher (1962), Kleffner (1962), and Bateman (1964), to name just a few. In general, these and other authorities agree that diagnosis must include assessment of performance level and identification of specific disability.

The specific standardized tests used in the diagnostic process vary considerably from examiner to examiner. Frequently broad-coverage tests, such as the Stanford-Binet Intelligence Scale, Wechsler Intelligence Scale for Children, and the Illinois Test of Psycholinguistic Abilities, are given first, followed by more specific instruments in those areas of difficulty revealed by the comprehensive tests. An exhaustive discussion of available standardized instruments would be overwhelming. The tests enumerated in this chapter are some of the most frequently utilized for assessment of the learning disabled.

Although there are numerous ways to categorize these tests, the following designations will be used: intelligence tests, visual motor/perceptual motor tests, language tests, auditory/verbal development and functioning tests, reading tests, and achievement tests.

INTELLIGENCE TESTS

Wechsler Intelligence Scale for Children (WISC)

The Wechsler Intelligence Scale for Children (Wechsler, 1949 a & b, 1955, for ages 5 through 15) was developed as a reaction against the age-scale format of the Stanford-Binet Intelligence Scale. Research has shown that the WISC is a reliable, stable, and valid instrument, correlating well with other individually and group-administered intelligence and achievement tests.

The Verbal, Performance, and Full Scale IQ's on the WISC are standard scores with means of 100 and standard deviations of 15. This procedure for calculating IQ's is particularly valuable so that IQ's at each age will be comparable throughout the range of the test.

Some of the major limitations of the WISC include: (1) limited applicability of norms for ages between 5 and 6 years, (2) limited range of IQ's (46-154), (3) difficulty in scoring responses, especially for the Comprehension, Similarities, and Vocabulary subtests, (4) limited applicability of norms to ethnic minority-group children, and (5) difficulties in interpreting subtest scores (Sattler, 1974).

Studies which have analyzed the scores of learning disabled children on the WISC are difficult to evaluate because the criteria employed to select children have differed among investigators. For those researchers who look at learning disabled children as underachievers, WISC scores tend to demonstrate higher results on the Performance Scale subtests than on the Verbal subtests, although Comprehension subtest scores may be higher than some Performance Scale subtest scores (Coleman and Rasof, 1963; Jenkins, Spivack, Levine, and Savage, 1964).

The lower scores are usually related to school-type learning tasks (e.g., Information and Arithmetic subtests).

36

When learning disabled children between 7 and 18 years old were classified as having neurological difficulty, having suspected neurological difficulty, or having no neurological difficulty, the three groups were not found to differ on their WISC scale scores or subtest scores (Boshes and Myklebust, 1964).

Dudek and Lester (1968), in a study using only the Verbal Scale, found individual differences on WISC subtest scores between adolescent underachievers and normal achievers to be small, although the underachievers had significantly lower scores overall than the normal achievers. Underachievers have more difficulty in concentration and attention tasks than normal achievers.

Researchers who classify reading disability under the category of learning disability have frequently utilized the WISC in their studies. However, many of the studies (Belmont and Birch, 1966; Lyle and Goyen, 1969) have suffered from methodological weaknesses including: (1) small sample size, (2) lack of control group, (3) difficulty in determining whether samples were representative of any definable population of readers, (4) failure to specify whether children have had any other associated dysfunction in addition to reading disability, (5) wide age ranges, and (6) uncontrolled sex ratios.

Because of the numerous methodological weaknesses present in the available studies, it is difficult to evaluate what, if any, WISC patterns are associated with retarded readers. Table 1 presents a sampling of some WISC studies done on children classified as learning disabled problem readers. The general trend emerging from these studies indicates that poor readers have a somewhat distinct pattern of WISC scores. A comparison done by Sattler (1974) of 22 such WISC studies (including most of those appearing in Table 1) indicates that the four easiest subtests for retarded readers are all Performance Scale subtests (Picture Completion, Picture Arrangement, Block Design, and Object Assembly) while three of the four most difficult subtests are Verbal Scale subtests (Information, Arithmetic, and Digit Span). In every

Table 1 WISC Studies on Learning Disabled/Problem Reading Children

Researcher(s) & Year	Number of Subjects	Description of Subjects	WISC Subtests on which LD/Problem Readers were Weak	WISC Subtests on which LD/Problem Readers were Strong
Graham, E. F. (1952)	31	All unsuccessful readers: Children between 8-0 and 16-11* who achieved either a verbal or performance IQ of 90 or higher who had fallen 25 percent or more below the mean reading level on the Wide Range Achievement Test (WRAT) and who had attended school	Arithmetic Vocabulary Coding	Similarities
Atlus, G. F. (1952)	25	Children referred to Guidance Department of the Santa Barbara Schools by their teachers because of their severe academic disabilities; full WISC IQ's of 80 or more	Coding Arithmetic Information	
Burks, H. F. Bruce, P. (1955)	31	Children classified as poor readers who were one or more years below grade level on the WRAT with WISC IQ's of 90 or above	Coding Information Arithmetic	Picture Arrangement Block Design Completion

*Ages written with dashes refer to a breakdown of years and months. For example, 16-11 refers to 16 years plus 11 months.

Table 1 WISC Studies on Learning Disabled/Problem Reading Children *(continued)*

Researcher(s) & Year	Number of Subjects	Description of Subjects	WISC Subtests on which LD/Problem Readers were Weak	Strong
Hirst, L. C. (1960)	30	All remedial reading cases with full scale IQ of 89 or above, reading 6 months below mental age; ages between 8-0 and 13-6	Arithmetic Digit Span	
Kallos, C. L. Grabow, J. M. Guarine, E. A. (1961)	37	All boys ages 9-14 with WISC IQ's of 90 to 109; each student at least two years retarded in reading achievement in relation to age expectation; no significant difference between verbal and performance IQ	Information Coding Arithmetic	Block Design
Neville, D. (1961)	70	35 of the children retarded two or more years in reading; 35 children not retarded in reading; all of the children with WISC IQ's of 90 or above and all male and matched in IQ, grade level, and sex	Information Arithmetic Digit Span Coding Similarities	Picture Arrangement Block Design

Table 1 *WISC Studies on Learning Disabled/Problem Reading Children (continued)*

Researcher(s) & Year	Number of Subjects	Description of Subjects	WISC Subtests on which LD/Problem Readers were	
			Weak	*Strong*
Robeck, M. (1964)	80	Elementary and junior high school children attending a reading clinic	Information Arithmetic Digit Span Coding	Comprehension Similarities Vocabulary Picture Completion Block Design
Coleman, J. C. Rasof, B. (1963)	293	177 successful readers and 116 backward readers age about 12½; analysis of covariance used for adjustment	Information Vocabulary Arithmetic Digit Span Coding	Picture Completion
Reid, W. R. Schoer, L. A. (1966)	87	Fourth-grade boys whose mean full scale WISC IQ's were in the 90 to 110 range; all social class effects nonsignificant	Arithmetic Digit Span Similarities	Picture Completion
Ackerman, P.T. Peters, J. E. Dykman, R. A. (1971)	116	82 children with specific learning disabilities and 34 controls with adequate academic performance	Arithmetic Digit Span Information Similarities	

one of the studies cited in Table 1 as well as in the 22 analyzed by Sattler, Verbal Scale IQ's are lower than Performance Scale IQ's.

Another method for analyzing the WISC scores of learning disabled children has been in terms of categories or group factors. Bannatyne (1968) used categories when analyzing the scores of genetic dyslexic readers. He defines this group as ". . . those persons (almost always male) who exhibit a syndrome of specific linguistic skill disabilities which restrict their ability to learn to read, spell, and write as well as their full scale intelligence would indicate" (p. 33). He refers to this group as "genetic" because of the amount of research evidence which indicates that the condition is inherited (Bannatyne, 1966). He has suggested that their WISC subtest scores are best analyzed in terms of categories he calls Spatial, Conceptual, and Sequential. Subtests of the Spatial category (Block Design, Object Assembly, and Picture Completion) require the ability to manipulate objects directly or symbolically in multidimensional space. Subtests in the Sequential category (Digit Span, Coding, and Picture Arrangement) require the ability to retain sequences of auditory and visual stimuli in short-term memory storage. Subtests in the Conceptual category (Vocabulary, Similarities, and Comprehension) require abilities more closely related to language functioning. Bannatyne (1971) reported that the genetic dyslexic readers receive their highest scores in the Spatial category, intermediate scores in the Conceptual category, and their lowest scores in the Sequential category.

Rugel (1974) reviewed 25 published and unpublished studies of the WISC subtest scores of disabled readers in terms of the Spatial, Conceptual, and Sequential categories. His findings agreed with those of Bannatyne. He considers Bannatyne's "genetic dyslexic" as a subclass of his (Rugel's) broader term "disabled reader" because he believes there are disabled readers who are not necessarily genetic dyslexics but who possess the same patterns.

Witkin, Dyk, Faterson, Goodenough, and Karp (1962), drawing upon the work of Cohen (1959), proposed that

41

WISC subtests fall into three major factors that tap relatively independent functions. In their scheme, a Verbal-Comprehension factor is composed of Information, Vocabulary, and Comprehension subtests; an Analytic-Field Approach factor is made up of Object Assembly, Block Design, and Picture Completion subtests; and an Attention-Concentration factor is composed of Arithmetic, Digit Span, and Coding subtests.

Keogh, Wetter, McGinty, and Donlon (1973), with a sample of 24 private-school children having serious learning and behavior problems and 26 boys referred to a pediatric learning disability clinic for evaluation of hyperactivity and learning problems, found that both learning disabled groups were adequate in the Verbal and Analytic abilities as classified by Witkin et al. However, their scores were lower on the Attention-Concentration items. This pattern was especially noticeable for children referred with a major complaint of hyperactive behavior.

Stanford-Binet Intelligence Scale
The Stanford-Binet Intelligence Scale (Terman and Merrill, 1960 a & b) is used with ages 2 through adult. The 1937 and 1960 forms of the Stanford-Binet have proved to be extremely reliable and valid instruments. However, the Stanford-Binet, like any measuring instrument, is far from perfect. The scales have been criticized for (a) placing too heavy emphasis on verbal and rote memory tests, (b) providing too few tests of g (i.e., general intelligence), (c) providing only one score (the IQ) to represent the complex nature of cognitive functions, (d) failing to measure creative abilities, and (e) being unsuitable for testing adults. Technical criticisms for all the Stanford-Binet forms include the cumbersomeness of the age-scale format, scoring and administration difficulties, and low ceiling for gifted adolescents.

On the Stanford-Binet, poor readers may demonstrate perceptual difficulty, poor recall of visual patterns, poor copying and reproduction of forms, and short memory span. Studying the child's pattern of successes and failures may provide clues to various kinds of cognitive difficulties. The

42

few available studies concerned with the performance of inadequate readers on the Stanford-Binet seem to support some of the above observations.

In one study, Bond and Fay (1950) matched 50 pairs of good and poor readers on mental age. The children were in grades 4, 5, and 6; using both the 1937 L and M Stanford-Binet forms, good readers performed better than poor readers on tests dependent upon the knowledge and use of words, while poor readers performed better than good readers on nonverbal and memory tests, but not consistently so.

Rose (1958) investigated the Stanford-Binet performance of a group of 113 poor readers who were between the ages of 6 and 17 years. All children in the sample had a reading level that was two years or more below expectancy. While statistical tests of significance were not performed nor control group used, the data point out trends which exist among the group of retarded readers.

The studies by Rose and by Bond and Fay confirm the expectation that poor readers tend to have more difficulty on the Stanford-Binet verbal tests than with other kinds of tests.

Slosson Intelligence Test (SIT)

The Slosson Intelligence Test (SIT) (Slosson, 1963, for ages 5 months through 27 years) was constructed to serve as an abbreviated form of the Stanford-Binet and to be used as a screening and retesting instrument. The SIT is an individual test of intelligence requiring 15 to 20 minutes to administer and score.

The test places heavy emphasis on language skills for children between 2 and 3 years of age; consequently, it may not be valid for children in this age group if they have delayed language development or are not from a middle-class environment (Hunt, 1972).

The SIT still maintains the ratio IQ, which has many disadvantages. The SIT manual reports correlations with the Stanford-Binet (Form L-M) ranging from .90 to .98 while correlations in other studies have ranged from .60 to .94 with a median correlation of .90. However, these correlations may be high because the Slosson contains items that are essentially adaptions from the Stanford-Binet. Correlations between SIT and WISC are uniformly higher with the Verbal Scale than with the Performance Scale.

The published research suggests that the SIT has merit as a quick screening device or perhaps as a device for retesting purposes. Advantages include the short administration time and relative ease of use by personnel with minimal training. The test, however, should not be used uncritically as a substitute for the Stanford-Binet, WISC, or other forms of the Wechsler Intelligence tests (Himelstein, 1972).

VISUAL MOTOR/PERCEPTUAL MOTOR TESTS

The Bender Visual Motor Gestalt Test

The Bender Visual Motor Gestalt Test (Bender, 1938, for all ages) purports to estimate the visual motor development of the child. Such development is seen as parallel to mental development and is associated with language ability (Bender, 1938). The test consists of nine designs, each on a separate card, which are presented one at a time to the child. He is requested to copy on a sheet of paper each successive design; no time limits are imposed. The reproduced designs are judged in terms of distortion, rotation, perseveration, method of reproduction, and other factors.

The Bender Visual Motor Gestalt Test seems to be one of the most frequent choices of diagnosticians in picking out the group of children with average or near-average intelligence who have a learning disability. The Bender is easy to administer, and the Koppitz scoring system (1964) allows the examiner to appraise the drawings of the children objectively and to estimate the child's developmental age. Thus the Bender has great appeal as a research and clinical instrument.

Poor performance in reproduction skills tested by the Bender have frequently been linked with learning disorders in children (Ames, 1969; Fisher, 1968; Keogh, 1969; and Koppitz, 1964). Ackerman, Peters, and Dykman (1971) studied the Bender protocols of 82 elementary school boys

44

with learning disabilities, scoring them for developmental error using the Koppitz system. Sixty-seven percent of the children with learning disabilities, as compared to only 44 percent of a group of 34 controls, made more errors than the mean for children of equivalent ages in Koppitz's normative sample.

Rotations either in the reproduction of design, in rotation on the paper, or in turning the cards have been studied by Chorost, Spivack, and Levine (1959), Goldberg (1959), Griffith and Taylor (1960), Havnik (1951, 1953), Koppitz (1958), and Clawson (1959). The results are equivocal in supporting the value of rotations in predicting brain damage. Most of these researchers suggest that the Bender test has some value as a screening device but that it should be used only with other data in making recommendations.

Longitudinal studies (Keogh, 1965; Keogh and Smith, 1967) based primarily on the Bender demonstrate that although there are consistent statistically significant relationships between Bender scores at kindergarten and later school achievement, caution must be used when making predictions about any particular child. Wedell (1970) added to this the belief that only in cases where severe disability is noted can later development be predicted from early perceptual motor functioning.

A recent study conducted by Coy (1974) fails to support the predictive value of the Bender Visual Motor Gestalt Test using the Koppitz scoring procedures for reading and math achievement of third-grade pupils. Coy hypothesizes it may be that the error is in the Koppitz scoring procedure, or it may be that the Bender is limited to a different age level not incorporated in Coy's study. He recommends extreme caution in using the Bender for identifying visual-motor deficiencies that have commonly been believed to be associated with poor reading and math achievement for third-grade pupils.

Although the Bender is usually given individually, Keogh and Smith (1961) demonstrated that it can be administered to groups of school beginners with the use of

45

large cards. They also showed that correlations with school achievement are higher for group than for individual administration. Keogh and Smith reported that children who performed well on the Bender in kindergarten tended to be good school performers but that poor Bender performance was nonpredictive.

Developmental Test of Visual-Motor Integration (VMI)

The Developmental Test of Visual-Motor Integration (VMI) was designed by K. E. Beery and N. A. Buktenica (1967) for ages 2 through 18. It consists of 24 designs in booklet form placed in an age-graded sequence as determined by normative studies with groups of children from ages 3 to 14. The classroom teacher can administer this test individually or to a group of students. Scoring is likewise done by the teacher.

A study conducted by Ryckman and Rentfrow (1971) concluded that the VMI possesses a sufficient degree of both test-retest and split-half reliability to merit its use with elementary school children. Chissom et al. (1972) points out that difficulties with the geometric form reproduction encountered in the past, such as the child's turning the individual piece of paper on which the geometric designs are reproduced from cards and thus changing the task, etc., have been alleviated through the booklet form of this test. He credits Beery and Buktenica with constructing the VMI according to sound theoretical consideration and methodological procedures.

Marianne Frostig Developmental Test of Visual Perception (DTVP)

Marianne Frostig (1964) has designed the Developmental Test of Visual Perception (DTVP), which can be used with ages 3 through 8. It was developed for the use of the classroom teacher on either an individual or group basis. This test, involving visuo-spatial and visuo-motor functions, has standardized these elements for (a) eye-motor coordination, (b) figure-ground, (c) form constancy, (d) position in space, and (e) spatial relations.

46

Chissom and Thomas (1971) notes that the authors of DTVP have based the test on a sound theoretical background coupled with experience they gained while working with the learning problems of children over a period of years.

Kephart (1972) states that " . . . within the area of visual perception, the Frostig Test probably yields the best information available today. If a child's score is low, it is likely he will have trouble in the classroom" (p. 1273). Smith and Marx (1972) caution against the indiscriminate use of the DTVP in schools without further investigation of its utility. (For other comments on the Frostig test, see chapter VIII.)

Purdue Perceptual-Motor Survey (PPMS)

The Purdue Perceptual-Motor Survey (PPMS) (Roach and Kephart, 1966) can be used with ages 6 through 11. It has as its objective the rating of perceptual-motor development. The survey consists of 30 items involving walking a board, jumping, identifying body parts, imitating movement, drawing, muscle tone and control, ocular pursuits, developmental drawing, and rhythmic writings.

Bannatyne (1971) evaluates the test manual as being well illustrated and the entire scale as being simple to administer. It appears to give results similar to other motor tests, particularly in the key areas of balance, fine motor movement, and coordination.

Jamison (1972) points out that it has not been significantly shown that the skills assessed by PPMS are necessary for academic learning nor even that particular levels are obtained by certain age groups. He maintains that this instrument should be used merely as one which allows the examiner to observe a series of perceptual motor behaviors and to isolate areas that may need further study.

Other Visual-Motor Tests

Other tests available for assessing visual-motor functioning include the following: Goodenough-Harris Drawing Test (GHDT, Harris, 1963, ages 3 through 15); Harris Test of

47

Lateral Dominance (1947, ages 7 through adult); Lincoln-Osertsky Motor Development Scale (Sloan, 1954, ages 6 through 14); Raven's Progressive Matrices Test (1965, ages 5 through adult); and the Memory-for-Designs Test (MFD, Graham and Kendall, 1960, ages 8-5 through adult). The phenomena under investigation are more specifically those of gestalt orientation; eye, hand, and foot dominance; eye-hand coordination, finger dexterity, gross and large muscle skills; visual discrimination; and brain damage, respectively. The reader should be cautious, however, in using the aforementioned tests, as research evidence supporting their measurement assumptions is somewhat lacking.

LANGUAGE TESTS

Types of Language Disabilities

Many learning disabled children have language problems. In a study of second-grade children with learning disabilities, Meier (1971) suggested that " . . . any investigation into the prevalence and characteristics of learning disabilities is primarily concerned with communication disorders" (p. 3). The nature of the communication problem varies and can affect all levels of language processing including perception, comprehension, formulation, and integration, as well as all aspects of language (phonologic, syntactic, and semantic). These areas of communication difficulty are evaluated by a speech pathologist. Often the speech pathologist has been involved in the assessment and therapy process for children whose speech is obviously disordered. However, many learning disabled children who have less obvious language problems also require evaluation.

Phonologic and syntactic problems have been the subject of vast research in communication disorders and are best understood. The nature of semantic deficits is less well known, but a text and several very excellent articles by Elizabeth Wiig and Eleanor Semel (1976, 1975, 1973) have provided new insight into problems learning disabled children have with cognitive processing of semantic aspects of audi-

48

tory language. They (Wiig and Semel, 1976) have identified the following areas of difficulty:
1. Semantic units (words and concepts)
2. Semantic classes (associations between related words and concepts)
3. Semantic relations (logical relations between words and concepts)
4. Semantic systems (verbal problems)
5. Semantic transformations (redefinitions of words and concepts)
6. Semantic implications (cause-effect relationships)

Use of Standardized Tests

Evaluating language disabilities in learning disabled children is often a difficult and time-consuming task, particularly for cases in which language deficits are primarily semantic. In children with phonologic and syntactic problems, language deficits are more obvious. Several well-known and standardized tests are available for such an evaluation. In addition, because these children have more obvious deficits, they can be identified early, well before school, so that appropriate language remediation can be provided. Early identification of language disabilities is important because of the implications of such disabilities for beginning reading and learning arithmetic concepts. According to Wiig and Semel (1976), academic areas of learning are affected by language disabilities.

There is no single standardized battery of tests for evaluating language and speech development. Speech pathologists select from several possible tests the ones which will best analyze the aspect of language they are evaluating. Often the battery is composed of a few short tests and several subtests from longer tests. Materials are chosen according to the age of the child, the modality of input or output, and the level of language processing. Occasionally a speech pathologist will administer a general test or do a screening to determine what deficits need further exploration.

Table 2 lists some available tests according to aspect of

49

Table 2 *Language Tests*

	Auditory (Decoding)	Speech (Encoding)
Phonology:	*Perception*	*Articulation*
	Wepman Auditory Discrimination Test (See Auditory Perception Section.) (Wepman, 1958)	Goldman-Fristoe Test of Articulation (Goldman & Fristoe, 1969)
	Templin Picture-Sound Discrimination Test (Templin, 1957)	Templin-Darley Test of Articulation (Templin & Darley, 1960)
	Goldman-Fristoe-Woodcock Test of Auditory Discrimination (See Auditory Perception Section.) (Goldman et al., 1970)	
	ITPA: Sound Blending and Auditory Closure (Kirk & McCarthy, 1968)	
Syntax & Morphology:	*Comprehension*	*Formulation*
	Test for Auditory Comprehension of Language (Carrow, 1973)	Berko Experimental Test of Morphology (Berko, 1958)
	Assessment of Children's Language Comprehension (Foster, Giddan, & Stark, 1972)	Carrow Elicited Language Inventory (Carrow, 1974)

Table 2 Language Tests (continued)

	Auditory (Decoding)	Speech (Encoding)
Syntax & Morphology: (continued)	*Comprehension* Northwestern Syntax Screening Test: Reception (Northwestern University, 1969)	*Formulation* ITPA: Grammatic Closure (Kirk & McCarthy, 1968)
	Vocabulary Comprehension Scale (Bangs, 1975)	Developmental Sentence Scoring (Lee, 1974)
		Northwestern Syntax Screening Test: Expression (Northwestern University, 1969)
Semantics:	*Comprehension* Peabody Picture Vocabulary Test (Dunn, 1959)	*Formulation* ITPA: Auditory Association, Verbal Expression (Kirk & McCarthy, 1968)
	Engleman Basic Concepts Inventory (Engleman, 1967)	Boston Diagnostic Aphasia Exam: Visual Confrontation Naming, Responsive Naming (Goodglass & Kaplan, 1972)
	ITPA: Auditory Reception (Kirk & McCarthy, 1968)	
General Communication:	*Comprehension and Formulation* Illinois Test of Psycholinguistic Abilities (Kirk & McCarthy, 1968) Porch Index of Communicative Ability in Children (Porch, 1974)	

language (phonology, morphology, syntax, semantics), level of processing (perception, comprehension, formulation, articulation), and modality (auditory, speech).

Templin-Darley Test of Articulation
The Templin-Darley (Templin and Darley, 1960) can be used with ages 3 through 8. Nine articulation tests, a 50-item screening test, a 141-item diagnostic test, and a 43-item Iowa Pressure Articulation Test are included in this articulation test battery. Spontaneous and imitated response to pictures for younger children and sentences for older children are scored for correctness, consistency, and stimulability of articulation. The test was validated by comparing measures from the articulation test to listeners' estimates of articulation defectiveness. The correlation was .78. Test-retest reliability coefficients for the tests were .93 to .99. The test provides norms for children from 3 to 8 years and at the half year for ages 3 to 5 (3½, 4½). Cut-off scores are given as guidelines for therapy decisions. As with any articulation test, results should be compared with articulation in conversational speech.

Test for Auditory Comprehension of Language (TACL)
The Carrow Test for Auditory Comprehension of Language (TACL) (Carrow, 1973, for ages 3 through 6-11) provides a developmental level for the comprehension of language structure. This is a broad test of comprehension of linguistic form classes, function words, morphological endings, grammar, and syntax. The test was validated by comparing its developmental levels with language acquisition in normal children. The test provides mean scores and standard deviations for Spanish and English-speaking white as well as black children at four age levels.

The TACL requires about 20 minutes to administer. Its results give a developmental age level score which should be interpreted in comparison with performance on the Peabody Picture Vocabulary Test, Assessment of Children's Language Comprehension, or other tests of language comprehension.

Assessment of Children's Language Comprehension (ACLC)
The Assessment of Children's Language Comprehension test (ACLC) (Foster, Giddan, and Stark, 1972) can be used with ages 3 through 6-5. It evaluates language comprehension and auditory memory of basic single-word vocabulary items and syntactic units two, three, and four elements long. The test was standardized on 3- to 6.5-year-old children, but it is not intended to be used to derive a developmental age for language comprehension. The test can be used to identify memory problems for certain grammatic forms. It is also intended as a guideline for beginning therapy.

The ACLC is short and can be administered in 10 to 15 minutes. It is most useful for very young children who are apt to have comprehension and memory problems. The test is appropriate for children with learning disorders because lexical items are presented in units, making possible the identification of the level at which a child is unable to process.

Developmental Sentence Scoring
The Developmental Sentence Scoring (Lee, 1974) can be used with ages 2-0 through 6-11. This is an objective measure of the syntactic development of children's oral language. The procedure is based on the comparison of children with suspected language disorders to children with normal development. The procedure has been statistically verified for reliability and validity (Koenigsknecht, 1974).

Developmental sentence analysis is based on analysis of a corpus of utterances. For children at a pre-sentence utterance stage of development, 100 utterances are transcribed and compared quantitatively and qualitatively to a chart of normal sentence types. For children speaking in sentences, 50 utterances are transcribed and scored in eight categories of grammatical forms, yielding a developmental sentence score. The developmental sentence score has been analyzed for the effect of age on development of the eight grammatical categories (Koenigsknecht, 1974). The results indicate that these categories show the most significant developmental progression by age. Developmental sentence analysis can be used on

53

speaking children of any age, but normative data reflect language use between 2 and 6 years, 11 months of age.

Northwestern Syntax Screening Test (NSST):
Expressive Portion
The Expressive Portion of the Northwestern Syntax Screening Test (Northwestern, 1969) can be used with ages 3 through 8. This is a screening instrument intended to provide an estimate of syntactic comprehension and expression. There are 20 sentences in each section for receptive and expressive testing. The test contains pictures which are described by the examiner for the child to subsequently identify or describe. The expressive section of the test requires the child to imitate a sentence about a picture. Psycholinguistic research has indicated that a child's ability to imitate sentences is one measure of his control of grammatical production (Brown and Bellugi, 1964).

The NSST is not a complete test of all common grammatical forms. Its intended purpose is identifying children whose syntactic capabilities should be further tested.

Normative data are provided. The test was standardized on 242 children. Percentile scores at six-month intervals are provided for both sections.

Peabody Picture Vocabulary Test (PPVT)
The Peabody Picture Vocabulary Test (PPVT) (Dunn, 1959, for ages 2-5 through 18) is a nonverbal, multiple-choice test designed to evaluate children who have no hearing disabilities and who can indicate "yes" or "no" in some manner. The test is untimed; it requires no reading ability, and neither pointing nor oral response is essential. Testing time is between 10 and 15 minutes. If the child cannot point, the examiner can administer the test by pointing to each picture and asking the child to designate whether it is correct or incorrect by some signal. These qualities make the test suitable for testing a variety of exceptional children (Bice and Cruickshank, 1966).

Sattler (1974), in a comparison of 14 studies on the reliability of the PPVT, found a median reliability score of .77. In a comparison of 37 concurrent validity studies between the Stanford-Binet and the PPVT, Sattler (1974) found a median correlation of .66.

The PPVT scores should not be considered in isolation from other measures of intelligence or of language ability (Ali and Costello, 1971). Special care must be given in examining ethnic minority group children because they have been found to obtain lower scores on the PPVT than on other intelligence tests.

Overall, reviews (Lyman, 1965; Piers, 1965) have found the test to be attractive, simple to administer, and easy to score. Piers observed that it is probably the best of its kind.

ITPA: Auditory Association, Verbal Expression

This subtest of the Illinois Test of Psycholinguistic Abilities (Kirk and McCarthy, 1968) is appropriate for ages 2-10 through 11 years. Children are given four common objects and asked to tell the examiner a number of things about the objects. In a pretest demonstration children are encouraged to provide information about the following attributes: (1) name, (2) color, (3) shape, (4) composition, (5) function or action, (6) major parts, (7) numerosity, (8) other physical characteristics, and (9) comparison. Syntax is not scored. Children are given points only for their semantic formulation. The test requires an understanding of the concept of classes of attributes as well as a vocabulary of words to designate these classes. Children who have memory deficits preventing them from logically grouping classes of words will have difficulty with this test.

When this test is administered as a subtest rather than as part of the total ITPA, the only readily interpretable score is the psycholinguistic age. This can be compared with the child's chronological age to determine whether he performed at age level. Psycholinguistic age subtest scores should not be used to make comparisons between or among other tests or subtests of the ITPA.

55

ITPA: Auditory Association

The Auditory Association subtest of the ITPA (Kirk and McCarthy, 1968) can be used with ages 2-4 through 10-11. It is a test of analogies. Children must understand an expressed analogy, e.g., "A rabbit is fast," and provide a word for a phrase that expresses a similar analogy, e.g., "A turtle is _____ " (Kirk and McCarthy, 1968, p. 37).

Items become increasingly more difficult as the test progresses. Wiig and Semel (1976) consider this a test of semantic relations. Children who do poorly on this test may have problems understanding and formulating verbal associations or recalling the key words of the given analogy. Wiig and Semel (1976) report that performance on this test correlates positively with PPVT and the comprehension of syntactic structure aspect of the NSST.

Illinois Test of Psycholinguistic Abilities (ITPA)

The Illinois Test of Psycholinguistic Abilities (Kirk and McCarthy, 1968, for ages 2 through 10) samples the child's abilities across the whole sensory-psychological communication system. According to Bannatyne (1971), the ITPA is not only well founded on a theoretical model, but it also is a very pragmatic assessment of the child's abilities. The ITPA, which takes 45 to 60 minutes to administer, yields 11-13 scores on such areas as auditory reception, visual closure, sound blending, etc. It has been found to be useful in determining the child's deficit areas in language functioning. The ITPA is a powerful tool for both the school psychologist and the remedial teacher when they wish to prescribe a work program for reading disability cases.

Hirshorn (1969), in a study done on 40 caucasian kindergarten children, concluded that the total language score of the ITPA, at least at the kindergarten level, is as valid a predictor as is the Stanford-Binet IQ for school achievement two years later.

Weener, Barnitt, and Melvyn (1967), in a critical evaluation of the ITPA, point out that there was a very selective

56

sample used in the standardization process (those with IQ's less than 80 and over 120 were excluded as were those with serious sensory or physical handicaps, blacks, and parochial school students). The result of this sampling is that there is a lack of a bottom or top on the ITPA for the lower or upper ranges of children. Weener et al. conclude that a range of abilities is assessed by the ITPA and that it can become a useful instrument as empirical evidence is provided to show how subscale performance is related to educationally related behaviors.

Choice and Results of Tests
Most of the language tests that have been described are not difficult to administer. However, the choice of tests and sub-tests to be used in an evaluation battery and the interpretation of the child's responses are neither simple nor straight-forward procedures. The test battery should be chosen according to what the test tasks will reveal. The examiner should know the tests' limitations and interpret accordingly. The results of testing should specify the problem areas of language and the level of language difficulty. In her interpretation, the examiner should discuss the implications of the child's particular language problem for his performance in various academic subject areas.

AUDITORY/VERBAL DEVELOPMENT AND FUNCTIONING TESTS

Auditory Perception Problems
Many children with learning disabilities have difficulties with auditory perception. Poor auditory perception has implications for language development, speech, and reading, although the specific auditory skills necessary for each area have not been identified. Auditory skills for learning language and learning to speak are probably quite different from auditory skills for learning sound-letter correspondences. Speech discrimination is the auditory skill most often studied with

children who have articulation difficulties. Results of that research indicate that there is no evidence for a general perceptual deficit. Dyslexic children have also been evaluated for their auditory discrimination abilities. Many perform quite adequately on the measures of auditory discrimination used in testing.

Nature of Auditory Perception

Research in speech perception of infants and adults indicates a maturational development. A slow progression of the development of adult perceptual strategies has been noted in young children. This development reflects a kind of hierarchy of task complexity. Chalfant and Scheffelin (1969) have analyzed auditory perception and have broken it into several tasks. Those are: (1) attention to auditory stimuli; (2) differentiation of sound versus no sound; (3) sound localization; (4) discrimination of phonemes; (5) discrimination of sound sequences; (6) auditory figure-ground selection; and (7) association of sounds with sources. Normally these components of auditory processing are part of a parallel process for simultaneous analysis of the features of a spoken message. Children with impaired language, defective articulation, or reading disabilities may have difficulty with more complex perceptual tasks, such as discrimination or sound sequences, or they may have trouble with more basic skills, such as attention. How each skill affects language learning and reading in normal children is not known. In addition, breakdown in any one of the categories involved in auditory perception abilities cannot be considered a cause of language or reading failure.

Evaluation of Specific Categories

Few standardized tests are available for evaluating each of the foregoing areas of auditory perception. Evaluation of speech perception abilities is most valuable since few inferences can be made about auditory perception from the perception of nonspeech (Rees, 1973). Major components of auditory perception that can be tested are auditory discrimination, auditory memory, and auditory segmentation. Auditory blending

58

and synthesis also are tested. Performance on these tasks is affected by the child's age, the meaningfulness of the material, phonemes tested, and the type of judgment the child is to make. In addition, research studies have found that task performance varies according to sex, intelligence, and socioeconomic conditions.

Some of the major tests available for evaluating components of auditory perception are shown in Table 3.

Table 3 Evaluation of Auditory Perception

Perceptual Skills Evaluated	Specific Auditory Perception Tests
Auditory Discrimination	Wepman Test of Auditory Discrimination (Wepman, 1958)
	Goldman-Fristoe-Woodcock Test of Auditory Discrimination (Goldman et al., 1970)
	Boston University Speech Sound Discrimination Picture Test (Pronovost & Dumbleton, 1953)
Auditory Blending	ITPA: Sound Blending (Kirk & McCarthy, 1968)
Auditory Closure	ITPA: Auditory Closure (Kirk & McCarthy, 1968)
Segmentation	Test of Auditory Analysis Skills (Rosner, 1975)

Before any of the tests in Table 3 are given, hearing acuity should be evaluated by an audiologist or a speech pathologist using standard pure tone air and bone conduction testing techniques. An informal interpretation of hearing acuity based on classroom observation is not adequate.

Brief descriptions of a few of the tests follow.

Wepman Auditory Discrimination Test
J. Wepman (1958) has developed the Wepman Auditory Dis-

59

crimination Test which can be used for ages 5 through 8. Because the ability to hear large and small differences between phonemes (sound units) is an aspect of phonological (sound system) development, this instrument also has been classified as a phonological test. The Wepman Auditory Discrimination Test presents 40 phonological oppositions (sound contrasts) in initial, medial, and final word position. Children make same-different judgments. The test has been widely used; however, there are some limitations to its identification of auditory discrimination problems. Some young children have difficulty understanding the concepts of same and different and may do poorly because of the judgment task. Some of the test's vocabulary is not familiar to young children. According to Wiig and Semel (1976), the scoring range is too narrow, and some consonant blends and vowels are not well represented. It is possible for some children with auditory discrimination problems to do well on this test.

Goldman-Fristoe-Woodcock Test of Auditory Discrimination
The Goldman-Fristoe-Woodcock Test of Auditory Discrimination (Goldman et al., 1970) can be used with ages 3 through adult. There are three parts to this test: (1) a training procedure, (2) auditory discrimination in quiet subtest, and (3) auditory discrimination in noise subtest. Both subtests are presented on tape. The background noise is cafeteria sounds. Stimulus items are pictured, four to a page. Words are all consonant-vowel or consonant-vowel-consonant one-syllable words. Words are paired so that the stimulus and the sample words differ by one phoneme. The phonemes that differ are in the same word position. The child is familiarized with each word in the test during a training session. During testing the stimulus word is named, and the child selects by pointing. The child with a learning disability is most apt to have difficulty on the auditory discrimination in noise subtest since this requires tuning out background sounds. Young children may have difficulty with the test vocabulary, even though they are given a training session. Since many of the vocabulary words are new, the child may forget them during the

test. The results of this test should be compared to articulation test results since this test is also a measure of phonological development.

ITPA: Auditory Blending
This subtest of the ITPA (Kirk and McCarthy, 1968) can be used with ages 2 through 10. It is a test of children's ability to synthesize phoneme sequences into words or nonsense syllables. The child must produce a word or syllable after hearing the sound units of the word or syllable spoken segmentally. The usefulness of this test is limited by the artificial nature of the task. Segmenting words or syllables in speech is difficult to do because of coarticulation (overlapping of sounds during production). This requires the child to identify a signal not usually encountered in speech production or perception.

ITPA: Auditory Closure
The Auditory Closure subtest of the ITPA (Kirk and McCarthy, 1968, ages 2 through 10) requires identification of a whole word from a part of a word. Words are spoken to the child with one or more phonemes deleted. Wiig and Semel (1976) report low five-month stability coefficients and an effect of age on internal consistency.

Test of Auditory Analysis Skills
The Test of Auditory Analysis Skills (Rosner, 1975, ages 5 through 8) is a screening measure of a child's ability to discriminate phonemic and syllabic segments of whole words. The child is presented with 13 words and asked to say the word with one element missing, e.g., "Say meat," "Say it again but don't say (m)." Although normative data are provided, Rosner's text did not describe standardization techniques of evaluation of validity and reliability.

READING TESTS
Because of the vast number of reading tests, only short synopses of the most popular ones are given as follows.

The Durrell Analysis of Reading Difficulty (Durrell, 1955) can be used with Grades 1 through 6. It is a battery of diagnostic tests designed to help in analysis and evaluation of specific reading difficulties.

The Gates-McKillop Reading Diagnostic Tests (Gates and McKillop, 1962) can be used with Grades 1 through 9. It is a battery of tests for individual administration designed to give diagnostic information about a child's reading skills.

The Gray Oral Reading Test (Robinson and Gray, 1963) is for Grades 1 through 6 and adults. It is an individually administered oral reading test which combines rate and accuracy to obtain grade level score.

ACHIEVEMENT TESTS

A very brief description of several achievement tests follows.

The California Achievement Tests (Tiegs and Clark, 1957) can be used with Grades 1.5 through 12. They form a battery of group tests to assess several areas of academic achievement.

The Metropolitan Achievement Tests (Durost et al., 1958, 1959) are appropriate for Grades kindergarten through 9.5. This battery of tests is group administered. It measures several areas of academic achievement: reading, spelling, arithmetic, etc.

The Stanford Achievement Test (Kelly, Madden, Gardner, and Rudman, 1966) for Grades 1.5 through 9.9 are group tests of academic achievement including reading.

The Wide Range Achievement Test, revised edition (Jastak and Jastak, 1965) can be used with ages 5 through adult. It is a brief individual test of word recognition, spelling, and arithmetic computation.

LIMITATIONS OF STANDARDIZED TESTS

Standardized tests may be useful for indicating specific areas of deficit; unfortunately, they do not often provide the critical, detailed information upon which an educational strategy can be based for an individual child. What is being measured and interpreted by most standardized psychological tests is performance which is neither sufficiently nor directly related to classroom behavior on assigned tasks. The Koppitz scoring procedure for the Bender, the Wechsler Intelligence Scale for Children, the Illinois Test for Psycholinguistic Abilities, and other commonly used diagnostic instruments do tap some overlapping, intertwining variables of school performance. Yet, evaluations and recommendations from such data rarely permit direct programming to alter the original school complaint. A child's inability to copy from the blackboard, to sit still, to name his letters, or to write his name is a highly individualistic performance not sufficiently explained by, or understood from, any single test or combination of tests presently available (Novack, Bonaventura, and Merenda, 1973).

Other problems exist with standardized tests. Children, especially children with learning disorders, vary markedly in day-to-day performance. What is thought to be an extremely disabling visual-motor deficit, as evidenced in an ITPA profile of one week, could vanish and be hardly detectable two weeks later. To be removed from class, led by the hand down the hall into an examination room, introduced to a stranger who is going to do something that is not quite understood, and then to be left alone is indeed an extraordinary and threatening experience for a child. Thus behavior exhibited may be quite different from that displayed in the classroom.

Besides changes in the subject's behavior, examiner variability is a further area of concern. Even a highly trained examiner is error susceptible. A completed WISC protocol was given to psychologists in training, all of whom had completed the appropriate course work. These individuals scored the protocol in a most dissimilar fashion; the resultant full scale IQ's ranged evenly from 76 to 93 (Miller, Chansky, and Gredler, 1970).

Hammill (1971) cites deficiencies in standardization populations as another weakness of standardized tests. In test manuals, item analyses, validity, and reliability coefficients, as well as administration procedures are meticulously reported, but they are generally based on the performance of "normal" or "representative" youngsters—the very children with whom the tests are never used. For example, the ITPA is devoid of both bright and dull pupils; the Frostig sample included no lower-class or black children. Even when the sample reflects the general population, there is little evidence that any standardized test will be appropriate for children who are called mentally retarded, hyperactive, perceptually handicapped, learning disabled, etc.

Hammill maintains that the validities and reliabilities of standardized tests are affected when the instruments are used with learning problem children or other "exceptional" children. For example, if the IQ of the sample declines, the validity and reliability coefficients are reduced correspondingly. Usually no mention of this is made in test manuals. Subsequently examiners continue to interpret subtests as if the standardization data reported in the manual were accurate. Two studies cited by Hammill (Baumeister and Bartlett, 1962; Osborne and Tillman, 1967) involve the factor analysis of the WISC using normal and mentally retarded children. Different factor structures emerged. This evidence supports Hammill's contention that procedures for interpretation of subtest results may be different for different samples of children.

SUMMARY

There are so many standardized tests available it would be impossible to cover all of them here. In this chapter brief synopses have been presented for the following tests:

  I. Intelligence Tests
      A. Wechsler Intelligence Scale for Children (WISC)
      B. Stanford-Binet Intelligence Scale
      C. Slosson Intelligence Test (SIT)
 II. Visual Motor/Perceptual Motor Tests
      A. Bender Visual Motor Gestalt Test for Children
      B. Koppitz scoring procedure (see Bender)
      C. Developmental Test of Visual-Motor Integration (VMI)
      D. Marianne Frostig Developmental Test of Visual Perception (DTVP)

    E.   Purdue Perceptual-Motor Survey (PPMS)
    F.   Goodenough-Harris Drawing Test (GHDT)
    G.   Harris Test of Lateral Dominance
    H.   Lincoln-Osertsky Motor Developmental Scale
    I.   Raven's Progressive Matrices Test
    J.   Memory-for-Designs Test (MFD)

III. Language Tests

    A.   Templin-Darley Test of Articulation
    B.   Test for Auditory Comprehension of Language (TACL)
    C.   Assessment of Children's Language Comprehension (ACLC)
    D.   Developmental Sentence Scoring
    E.   Northwestern Syntax Screening Test (NSST), Expressive Portion
    F.   Peabody Picture Vocabulary Test (PPVT)
    G.   ITPA: Auditory Association, Verbal Expression
    H.   ITPA: Auditory Association
    I.   Illinois Test of Psycholinguistic Abilities (ITPA)

IV. Auditory/Verbal Development and Functioning Tests

    A.   Wepman Auditory Discrimination Test
    B.   Goldman-Fristoe-Woodcock Test of Auditory Discrimination
    C.   ITPA: Auditory Blending
    D.   ITPA: Auditory Closure
    E.   Test of Auditory Analysis Skills

V. Reading Tests

    A.   Durrell Analysis of Reading Difficulty
    B.   Gates-McKillop Reading Diagnostic Tests
    C.   Gray Oral Reading Tests

VI. Achievement Tests

    A.   California Achievement Tests
    B.   Metropolitan Achievement Tests
    C.   Stanford Achievement Test
    D.   Wide Range Achievement Test (Revised Edition)

Standardized tests yield useful information about the child's level of functioning, but they do not provide information on educational procedure. They also do not measure the variability of daily performance or the effect the testing environment has on performance.

Standardization populations may not be applicable to the exceptional child. At the upper and lower ends of the scale, the tests may lose their validity.

Because formal standardized tests are to be administered on a one-to-one basis and are very lengthy, it has been necessary to develop shorter tests which can be given to large numbers of children in succession. These are meant only to identify those children who may be having difficulty so they may be more thoroughly evaluated.

CHAPTER 5 DETECTION THROUGH SCREENING BATTERIES

THE BATTERY APPROACH
In an effort to find an approach faster than administering such tests as the WISC, ITPA, Wepman, etc., researchers have been developing screening batteries. In many cases they are composed of only portions of the standardized tests. The batteries are especially powerful as screening tools because they select out of the standardized tests subtests that are the best identifiers of learning problems.

The battery approach to screening learning disabilities often utilizes a station system in which the child being tested moves from place to place (one station to the next) and is tested on a different skill at each location. Many of the batteries reported are in the experimental stages. Time is the big factor needed to see how reliably these tests identify high-risk cases. (See Table 4 at the end of this chapter.)

SCREENING BATTERIES IN USE

Predictive Index
One of the outstanding efforts in developing tests predictive

of learning problems is that of de Hirsch, Jansky, and Langford (1965). The primary purpose of their study is to produce a prognostic test battery that identifies at kindergarten age those children who are high risks for later failure in reading, spelling, and writing. A test battery was administered to kindergarten-age subjects and was followed by a second battery of tests given to the subjects when they completed second grade. About one-half of the predictor tests correlated significantly with the second-grade achievement. The group constructed the de Hirsch Predictive Index consisting of those combined tests that most effectively identified the high-risk children. The 10 tests in the Index were the Bender Visual Motor Gestalt Test; the Wepman Auditory Discrimination Test; Number of Words Used Telling a Story, Category Names, and Pencil Use (de Hirsch et al., 1965); Horst Reversals Test (1958); and Word Matching, Word Recognition I and II, and Word Reproduction subtests of the Gates Reading Readiness Inventory (1939). The Index not only identified 10 of 11 disabled readers or spellers in the project, but it also singled out two children who were superior.

Adkins et al. (1971), in a factor analysis of the de Hirsch Predictive Index, conclude that the battery to a large extent is tapping a major visual discriminatory component of the 5½-year-old subject. They find this visual discriminative behavior interlocked with progressively more complex processes that begin with fine motor coordination predictions (Bender), moving to identification (Horst Reversals) and classification (Categories), and finally to immediate memory for complex visual symbols (Word Reproduction).

Developmental Indicators for the Assessment of Learning

Developmental Indicators for the Assessment of Learning (DIAL) is a one-year project, which has been carried out in Illinois through Title VI to develop a screening procedure for identification of pre-kindergarten children with potential learning disorders (Mardell and Goldenberg, 1972). The assessment of each major area of functioning is assigned to a "station" with evaluation completed by a previously trained "operator." In the assessment process (after having his picture taken), the child progresses through the various stations: gross motor, fine motor, conceptual, and communications. At each station the operator notes the child's performance with a circle or slash on a single score sheet that follows him from place to place. The entire procedure takes 25 to 30 minutes per child. Emphasis is placed on instruments applicable to children 2½ to 5½ years.

The designers point out several useful aspects of this screening procedure. The child is dealt with on a one-to-one basis at a minimal cost. Well-trained professionals and/or well-trained paraprofessionals may administer the test. In addition, the team approach removes dependence upon singular judgments.

Union, New Jersey, Screening Program

The program instituted by the Board of Education, Union, New Jersey (1968), has as its goals identification of all first-grade children who have a developmental lag in any area of perception (i.e., gustatory, olfactory, tactile, kinesthetic, auditory, visual) or any youngster who appears to have adequate functioning sensory channels but has not learned to integrate and synchronize these modalities or systems in order to function efficiently.

The screening process consists of tests on postural-transport orientations (gross motor coordination), auditory dynamics, association processes, and perceptual-motor match. Children are further tested for auditory and visual acuity as well as for oculomotor imbalance. The process allows for four children to be screened per hour, spending 15 minutes at each of four stations. Some of the standardized instruments utilized at the various stations are Goodenough Draw-A-Man Test (Goodenough, 1926), ITPA Auditory Vocal Sequencing Test, and ITPA Auditory Vocal Association Test. These are combined with more informal evaluative devices such as simple improvised commands, clapping patterns, and body identification. Those students scoring in the lowest 5 percent of one or more of these subtests as well as in

69

the lowest 10 percent of the total scores are designated candidates for intensive perceptual training.

The children are screened during the summer prior to admittance into school. Mothers who accompany their children are occupied in the following ways: (1) viewing videotape demonstration of perceptual motor training, (2) filling out forms about their socioeconomic status and experiential background of the child, and (3) being interviewed by a psychologist concerning the birth and developmental history of the child.

Project Genesis (Title III Grant)
Jens (1970), with a Title III grant, set up Project Genesis, a preventive program whose purpose was to identify potential learning deficiencies before children enter kindergarten and to provide individual programming to offset future learning problems. Clinics, held in the spring, test each child entering kindergarten. According to Jens (1970), the cost is less than $.035 per child (printing). The process takes less than 45 minutes per child and utilizes mother volunteers. Five stations are set up: (1) perceptual-motor, (2) vision, (3) hearing, (4) speech and language, and (5) psychological-developmental history. In addition to volunteer help, a speech therapist, school nurse, and school psychologist are at appropriate spots.

Jens concluded that (1) learning problems can be screened out, (2) parents are willing to act as volunteers, and (3) teachers do find time to work needed activities into their program. It must be emphasized that these procedures are meant only for screening and cannot be construed as substituting for professional visual, auditory, perceptual-motor, or psychological examinations!

Wizard of Oz Screening Program
A screening program was designed by Amundson (1972) for the purpose of discovering strengths and weaknesses in individual children prior to formal schooling. This was done since experiences in early education can pattern responses to an

acceptable level of accomplishment before formal schooling. The functioning of motor, visual, auditory, and language abilities are assessed.

The tests in the screening program are arranged around the theme from the *Wizard of Oz* story and movie. Some of the sources of the standardized items are the ITPA, Kephart Norms (Kephart, 1960), Marianne Frostig Developmental Test of Visual Perception, Ilg and Ames Readiness Battery (Ilg and Ames, 1964), and the de Hirsch Predictive Index. Evaluation centers on motor, visual, auditory, and language competencies. The program format specifies that children are individually occupied at each of 24 stations for a total of 45 minutes for each child. Volunteers manning the stations are parents, teenagers, and members of professional groups.

Advantages noted by Amundson are the early identification of problems, easy scoring, easy administration, short administration time, and, finally, the simple construction of the test.

Modified Predictive Index

Eaves, Kendall, and Crichton (1972) conducted a study which was the first phase of an attempt to standardize an instrument for screening all kindergarten children and identifying those expected to fail in school because of minimal brain dysfunction. The battery derived is called the Modified Predictive Index (MPI), consisting of 10 tests of the Predictive Index (de Hirsch et al., 1965), the Goodenough Draw-A-Man Test, and name printing.

Eaves et al. conclude that the MPI is a relatively quickly and easily administered measure that yields valuable predictive information about children who are in all other respects of human growth and development normal except for experiencing minimal brain dysfunction. It is practical for use with large numbers of children to identify those who definitely need some special attention. It was found that the test easily could be given by a public health nurse, remedial teacher, kindergarten teacher, or similar personnel after minimal training by a psychologist.

Skokie Screening Program

Skokie School District (1969), a Chicago suburban public school, has demonstrated a system-wide program for learning disabilities in grades 2 to 6. The identification phase of the program consists of two screens: one involving group tests and one utilizing an individual intelligence test. The screen rules out mental retardation, sensory deprivation, and serious primary emotional disturbances as causes of learning disability in the participants and isolates significant under-achievers by objective criteria. Screen I consists of the Alpha Form of the Otis Quick-Scoring Mental Ability Test (Otis, 1954) and the Stanford Achievement Tests. These were administered to all children at a given grade level in their classrooms. A screening list was compiled of those children underachieving in terms of their own ability according to selected criteria. These children were selected for further testing. For the first three grade levels, teachers were asked to nominate students who they thought had learning disabilities but did not appear on the list. Screen II was given to those identified as probable learning disability cases; it consists of individual intelligence tests and more achievement tests [WISC, Metropolitan Achievement Tests, Gates-MacGinitie Reading Tests (Gates and MacGinitie, 1972), and Picture Story Language Test (Myklebust, 1965)].

The two-screen identification program was found to be effective, identifying about 9.8 percent of the population as having mild to severe learning disabilities. Diagnostic teachers assembled all data accumulated about each pupil and made a tentative diagnosis of the problems. The final phase of the program included implementation of educational prescriptions.

Glenview, Illinois, Screening Program

District No. 34 in Glenview, Illinois, has developed a screening program for identifying children with potential learning problems during their kindergarten year (Plantz, 1972). The screening program being implemented district wide consists of the following steps. The first, or gross screening, is given to all kindergarten children. As a part of this process kindergarten teachers are asked to complete the Pupil Rating Scale (Myklebust and Boshes, 1969) for each child in their class. This instrument reviews the characteristics of the child in auditory comprehension, spoken language, orientation, motor coordination, and personal social behavior. A further part of the gross screen is the Screening Test for Academic Readiness (STAR) (Ahr, 1967) administered by learning development teachers. Children who score below pre-determined criteria are then screened intensively in the auditory, visual memory, and motor areas. After all evaluation, students who turn up with a problem are placed in one of the following categories: (1) learning disabled, (2) close watch, (3) emotional problems, (4) slow learners, and (5) socially immature. Appropriate recommendations are then made.

Classroom Screening Instrument
Meier (1971), under the auspices of the Rocky Mountain Educational Laboratory, has developed the Classroom Screening Instrument (CSI) to be used by teachers to pick out high-risk cases in terms of individual learning disabilities. The instrument was further designed to provide significant data for diagnosticians, school psychologists, etc., who might be called upon to conduct in-depth evaluations of the high-risk pupils.

In validating the instrument, Meier's sample was taken from eight Rocky Mountain states and included 80 classroom teachers meeting a specified criterion - at least one year of satisfactory experience as a second-grade classroom teacher (art and music teachers were also included). The program uses three levels of screening. In Level I these teachers administered a uniform spelling test, a pupil productions fill-in sheet, a design-copying test, and the Goodenough Draw-A-Man Test (Goodenough, 1926) to the students in their classes. Teachers then identified those children who were having unusual difficulty in learning by ranking them. Next, each teacher filled out the Classroom Screening Instrument on each child. The 80 behavioral indices of the CSI are checklist items of an essentially eclectic grouping of observable behavior previously designated as at least symptomatic of individual learning disabilities. The most noteworthy data regarding the CSI are the number of times the teachers checked the various behavioral indices for the 284 children who subsequently were diagnosed as bona fide learning disability cases.

A Level II screen was given to those subjects who, under pre-established criteria, qualified as probable learning disability candidates. Tests administered included the WISC, Wide Range Achievement Test, Developmental Test for Visual-Motor Integration, Developmental Test of Visual Perception (Frostig), ITPA, Templin-Darley Test of Articulation, and standard pure tone audiometric screening.

The Level III screen included a medical diagnosis of those cases in which learning disability was highly suspected.

Conclusions by Meier were: (1) classroom teachers are successful in accurately making a screening instrument; (2) scales are descriptive and highly discriminative, and (3) factor analysis and cluster analysis reveal that the original categories held up quite well in most instances.

See Table 4 for a review of screening batteries.

SUMMARY

The screening batteries described here are essentially adaptations of more lengthy formal standardized tests. The battery approach to screening for learning disability often utilizes the station system in which each station tests a different skill. Brief synopses are presented for the batteries listed in Table 4 in this chapter.

The battery approach has proved to be very effective in identifying children who may have future learning problems. This approach, however, suffers from the same type of problem as the formal standardized test—it is time consuming and allows only a few children to be tested in one testing session.

Table 4 Screening Batteries

Originator(s)	Instrument Name	Statement of Purpose	Age of Administration	Standardized Tests Utilized in Part or All *
de Hirsch, K. Jansky, J. J. Langford, W. S. (1965)	Predictive Index	Prognostic test which identifies kindergarten-age children who are high risk	Kindergarten	Bender Visual Motor Gestalt Test Wepman's Auditory Discrimination Test de Hirsch: (not standardized) Number of Words Used in Telling a Story, Category Names Horst Reversals Gates Reading Readiness Inventory: Word Matching I & II Recognition I & II Word Reproduction
Skokie School District No. 68 (1969)	Skokie Screening Program	Screen I: To rule out mental retardation, sensory deprivation, and serious emotional disturbances as a cause of the learning disability	Grade 2 to Grade 6	Screen I: Otis Quick-Scoring Mental Ability Test (Alpha Form) Stanford Achievement Tests

*See chapter 4 for references on standardized tests. Tests not cited in chapter 4 are referenced in the text of chapter 5 or chapter 6.

Table 4 Screening Batteries (continued)

Originator(s)	Instrument Name	Statement of Purpose	Age of Administration	Standardized Tests Utilized in Part or All *
Skokie School District No. 68 (1969) (continued)	Skokie Screening Program	Screen II: To identify the probable learning disability		Screen II: WISC Metropolitan Achievement Tests Gates-MacGinitie Reading Test Picture Story Language Test
Board of Education, Union, New Jersey (1968)	Union, New Jersey, Screening Program	Identification of all first-grade children who have a developmental lag in any area of perception	Grade 1	Goodenough Draw-A-Man Test ITPA: Auditory Sequencing ITPA: Auditory Vocal Association
Jens, D. (1970)	Project Genesis (Title III Grant)	Preventive program to identify potential learning deficiencies before kindergarten and make provision for individual programming	Pre-kindergarten	No standardized tests used in part or total

Table 4 Screening Batteries (continued)

Originator(s)	Instrument Name	Statement of Purpose	Age of Administration	Standardized Tests Utilized in Part or All *
Meier, J. H. (1971)	Classroom Screening Instrument (Rocky Mt. Ed. Lab.)	Screening technique used by teachers to identify high-risk cases in terms of individual learning disabilities	Age 7 through 8	Goodenough Draw-A-Man Test Pupil Productions Fill-In Sheet WISC Wide Range Achievement Test Developmental Test for Visual-Motor Integration Frostig Developmental Test of Visual Perception ITPA Templin-Darley Test of Articulation Standard pure tone screening
Mardell, C. A. Goldenberg, D. S. (1972)	Developmental Indicators for the Assessment of Learning (DIAL)	Identification of pre-kindergarten children with learning disorders	Pre-kindergarten	No standardized tests used in part or total

Table 4 Screening Batteries (continued)

Originator(s)	Instrument Name	Statement of Purpose	Age of Administration	Standardized Tests Utilized in Part or All *
Amundson, M. S. (1972)	Wizard of Oz Screening Program	Discovery of strengths and weaknesses in individual children before formal schooling	Pre-school	ITPA Kephart Norms Frostig Developmental Test of Visual Perception Ilg & Ames Readiness Battery de Hirsch Predictive Index
Eaves, L. C. Kendall, D. C. Crichton, J. (1972)	Modified Predictive Index (MPI)	Screening technique for kindergarten children to identify those expected to fail in school because of minimal brain dysfunction	Kindergarten	10 tests of de Hirsch's Predictive Index Goodenough Draw-A-Man Name printing
Plantz (1972)	Glenview, Illinois, Screening Program (District 34)	Identification of children with potential learning problems	Kindergarten	Pupil Rating Scale Screening Test for Academic Readiness

CHAPTER 6 DETECTION THROUGH SCREENING INSTRUMENTS

THE SCREENING APPROACH

The general consensus seems to be that the earlier a potential learning problem can be discovered, the more successful will be the remediation. What instruments, therefore, should be used to isolate the potential learning problem? What tests are most valid for the amount of time spent? This chapter will deal with individual screening instruments. They are group tests given usually by a single individual to a large group of children at one time. (See Table 5 at the end of this chapter.)

SCREENING INSTRUMENTS IN USE

Screening Test for Academic Readiness

Ahr (1967) recently reported on a group preschool screening instrument—Screening Test for Academic Readiness, or STAR—used in an upper-middle-class community and subsequently with Head Start programs. Correlations with individual and group intelligence and achievement tests compared favorably with the predictive coefficients of other group intelligence tests at this age level. The test can be administered in less than one hour, and it can be given to large groups of children simultaneously. The eight subtests of STAR are: human figure drawing, picture vocabulary, letters (recognition, printing), picture completion, copying geometric designs, picture description, relationships (size, space, direction, and position of mutilated pictures), and numbers. Five items involve copying, drawing, or printing; three involve multiple choice, and the subject chooses one drawing by outlining it with a pencil. Ahr's instrument, still in an experimental stage, systematically taps a variety of numerical, receptive verbal, visual-motor, and relational abilities.

Magoon and Cox (1969), administering the STAR to a nationwide sample of approximately 400 environmentally diverse subjects, conclude that with the exception of two subtests it is questionable whether a sufficient construct of factorial validity scores are derived from STAR subtests. The factor analysis has revealed what was judged to be a structure dimensionally unrelated to scholastic achievement. Magoon and Cox stated that the STAR's factorial does not fulfill many of the criteria for a school readiness measure as defined by developmental experts.

First Grade Screening Test
Pate and Webb (1966) have developed a group measure called the First Grade Screening Test (FGST), which can be administered at the end of the kindergarten year. This test is reported to identify young children with potential learning problems. Extensive validation and reliability information is given by the authors, according to Rogolsky (1968). The FGST can be administered to a kindergarten class by a teacher in about 45 minutes. The 27 items of the test are not categorized by the authors but can be grouped as follows: picture vocabulary (10 items), drawing and visual-motor functioning (5 items), social and practical perception and information (4 items), memory for pictures (2 items), following directions (2 items), and pictures which call on the child to identify with the well adjusted (4 items). No tests of num-

bers concepts are included. Many of the items in the FGST are similar to those in Ahr's STAR (see preceding discussion). The STAR's organization into subtests gives the examiner more detailed information than FGST's unitary score. Rogolsky (1968) has described the FGST as an attractive, easy-to-administer screening technique. Its standardization on a variety of populations is especially noteworthy.

Ransom (1969), in a critical evaluation of FGST, maintains that the instrument does not meet several specifications as named in the Standards for Educational and Psychological Tests (American Psychological Association, 1966). Ransom sums up his evaluation of the FGST by stating that "Although sufficient specific evidence of construct validity is lacking, this test does give empirical evidence of providing a quickly and simply administered test for identifying a good percentage of ending kindergarten or beginning first grade children who are 'high risks' for failure in academic work" (p. 37).

Slingerland Screening Tests for Identifying Children with Specific Language Disability

The Slingerland Screening Tests for Identifying Children with Specific Language Disability (1962) were developed for use with the second semester of the first grade and continuing through the fourth grade. The hypothesis behind these instruments is that early identification of maturational lags and the perceptual-motor disabilities that may cause school failure should result in appropriate educational intervention that will forestall failure.

The subtests of the SST's give evidence of maturational lag or deficits in the sensory-motor channels that subserve language learning. Because visual, auditory, and kinesthetic modalities are involved in varied associations through the eight subtests, relative strengths and weaknesses of those modalities may be assessed. Though not diagnostic instruments, the SST's do indicate when there is a need to refer children who give evidence of severe disability in the screening. Furthermore, in the absence of diagnostic facilities within the community, the teacher may use the instruments as a guide to appropriate intervention in the classroom. Anasara (1968) concludes that indeed the SST's may be useful tools in identifying learning problems.

Sapir Developmental Scale

The Sapir Developmental Scale (Sapir and Wilson, 1967) is a survey instrument to be used with a total kindergarten population and administered by a trained kindergarten teacher. The three major areas covered in this test are (1) perceptual-motor skills, including visual discrimination, visual memory, visual motor, auditory discrimination, and auditory memory; (2) bodily schema, including visual-motor-spatial, bodily image and directionality; and (3) language, including orientation as well as vocabulary. The testing time is 30 minutes maximum.

The Sapir Developmental Scale was validated in the following manner. It was administered in January of the kindergarten year to 54 children. During the fall of the first grade (a month after school started) the Marianne Frostig Developmental Test of Visual Perception was administered, followed a month later by the New York State Readiness Test. A year later neurologists examined the subjects, rating them on a 1-10 scale, with 5 signifying a borderline case. Norms of the Sapir Developmental Scale were established at 70 percent, classifying 18 of the subjects as developmentally deficient. The New York State Readiness Test and the Marianne Frostig Developmental Test of Visual Perception verified these findings ($p < .01$).

This study demonstrates that with *this* population, developmental differences are accurately identified at the kindergarten level; they persist in the first grade and correlate significantly with academic performance 17 months later. The Sapir Developmental Scale is slated to be used with a larger population, and the results will be studied to see whether the scores maintain the correlation with academic achievement.

82

Minnesota Percepto-Diagnostic Test

Fuller and Laird (1963) propose a single-factor approach to learning disability screening at all age levels. They have developed the Minnesota Percepto-Diagnostic Test (MPD), which they claim provides a rapid and objective method for determining whether the etiology of a reading disability is organic, primary, or secondary. The MPD consists of six gestalt designs which the subject copies. The reproduced designs are scored for degrees of rotation. Because the subject does not know the scoring technique, he cannot aim for correct responses. Because the test is culture free, the factors of education, intelligence, and reading ability, within limits, do not influence the results of the MPD.

The MPD has been standardized on more than 1,200 children and adults. It was found that an empirical progressive index of rotations was on a continuum from normalcy to abnormalcy so that the degree of rotation differentiates at a significance of .001 between adult normals, personality disturbed, and neurologically dysfunctional (Laird, 1962) and between normal children, emotionally disturbed, and schizophrenic as well as reading disabled (Fuller, 1962).

Bateman (1966) seriously questions the validity of the MPD. In standardizing the MPD, she points out, the Gates Primary Reading Test (Gates, 1926) that is designed for first grade and the first half of second grade is used on subjects with mean chronological age of 10 years, 3 months. Bateman discusses another questionable feature of the MPD. Before giving the test, the diagnostician must first decide to use the classification of reading disability or behavioral problem. For the behavioral problem category, 55 degrees of rotation indicates schizophrenic perception; if the reading disability classification is used, 55 degrees of rotation indicates organic reading disability. Similarly, 30 degrees of rotation can suggest either secondary reading disability or emotional disturbance.

Dyslexia Schedule

The Dyslexia Schedule (DS) was devised by McLeod (1966)

for the purpose of assessing predisposition for childhood dyslexia in first graders or with any child with reading difficulty. This predictive device is used as the nucleus of an interview between a social worker and the parents. The validation study was done in Brisbane, Australia, where the incidence of reading retardation was found to be low (3.25 percent as compared to 21 percent in Britain). As the researcher points out, it might be expected that incidence of dyslexia in the neurological or genetic sense would be relatively constant from culture to culture. Therefore, the child with reading retardation in Brisbane would be more likely to be dyslexic than would one in a place where the incidence of reading retardation is greater. McLeod found a significant difference between the experimental and control groups in 23 of the 90 original items. A large-scale investigation with this instrument is being planned to determine whether it can be used as a screening device.

Kling (1972), in a critical evaluation of the DS, faults McLeod on not "tightening up" his definition of the term "dyslexia" so that the results of the instrument would have more meaning. Besides a lack of criterion for the dyslexic, there is no adequate description of nondyslexics.

Meeting Street School Screening Test
The Meeting Street School Screening Test (MSSST) was developed to help identify children in kindergarten and first grade who had had cerebral dysfunction or neurological impairment (Denhoff, Siqueland, Komich, and Hainsworth, 1967). It is the result of 7 years of research in the area of learning disability and is based on experience with children showing a wide range of neurological difficulties. There are two versions. One is of primary interest to physicians; the other is designed for educators, psychologists, and other professionals concerned with the educational implications.

The physician's form is a 36-item test that can be added to the medical review of 6- to 7½-year-old patients (Denhoff, Siqueland, Komich, and Hainsworth, 1967). It is the result of blending the best items used by the pediatric neurologist and the various therapists. The items measure imbalance, poor coordination, inadequate gross and fine motor performance, lack of sensory awareness, as well as survey language skills. This test is designed to reduce the amount of subjectivity when physicians describe "soft" neurological signs (i.e., clumsiness). The need is great for school and community pediatricians to participate with school personnel in identifying and managing the young school-aged child with cerebral dysfunction or learning disabilities. This test helps to bridge the gap in this vital area of child health and education.

The other form of the MSSST (Hainsworth and Siqueland, 1969) was devised to have high reliability and validity and to be administered by teachers, psychologists, or even lay persons. It is an individually administered, 20-minute test to survey the child's developmental growth in the areas through which information is exchanged, and hence, learning occurs. This form of the MSSST is made up of three subtests that survey the child's skills in specific information processing. They are: (1) visual-perceptual-motor, (2) language, and (3) body awareness and control. The total score reflects the child's overall efficiency in information processing, whereas the three subtest scores reflect his skill in each of the modalities. The selected items are designed to cover intake, integration, and output skills within these modalities.

Inasmuch as no single criterion identifies the learning disabled population adequately, validity of the MSSST was assessed in three ways. (1) The first involves predicting later school achievement levels of kindergarten and first-grade children tested with the MSSST. Eighty percent of the children scoring below the median on the MSSST had school achievement scores below the median two years later. Many of the remaining 20 percent were bright learning disabled children who were rarely maintaining average grade placement. (2) In a collaborative study involving 178 children studied from birth through 7 years of age, the MSSST correlated significantly with indices reflecting the degree of neurological involvement of dysfunction. (3) The test discriminates between children with identified perceptual-motor and language handicaps and those from the normal population. It also correlates with longer diagnostic tests, such as the Marianne Frostig Developmental Test of Visual Perception and the Illinois Test of Psycholinguistic Abilities, further indicating that the MSSST provides an adequate screening of the skills tapped by these particular tests.

Neuro-Developmental Observation

The Program for Learning Studies at the Children's Hospital of D.C. and George Washington University School of Medicine has been developing protocols for diagnostic evaluation of learning problem children. These protocols emphasize the operational approach. An attempt is made to find out in time-limited diagnostic interaction what works in relation to the individual child.

Ozer and Richardson (1972), two physicians working in conjunction with this project, have selected a set of tasks which are suitable for diagnosis in the 5- to 8-year-old age group. The 15-minute examination protocol called the Neuro-Developmental Observation (NDO) is generally administered by a health professional. It is done as the basis for child-development counseling for the child's parent and/or teacher (Ozer and Richardson, 1972).

Three major groups of tasks exist within the NDO. The first illustrates breaking a task into a series of component parts. The second provides a series of instructions in which the modalities of presentation are varied as the child carries out a group of motor tasks. In the final section, the child engages in a drawing exercise.

The examination protocol illustrates a basic principle of the diagnostic process: The child's success in carrying out a task is affected by the intervention of the examiner.

The child's parent and/or teacher observes the entire evaluation. The report forms differ from standard referral forms because they are seen as a component of the process of making whatever seems "to work" meaningful to the parent or teacher observing the NDO. This observation offers an opportunity to better understand the difficulty by having

86

shared a common experience. The active involvement of all three (child, parent, and teacher) is aimed at the recognition of their competence and responsibility in developing an effective learning environment for the child.

Learning Problem Indication Index

Hoffman (1971) has developed a Learning Problem Indication Index (LPII) for the use of a physician to identify, as early as the age of 2, the child with low learning potential and to distinguish children whose academic failure results from a neurological dysfunction. The LPII presents a list of perinatal and developmental events which may be used as learning problem indicators.

Hoffman's study compares the perinatal and developmental history of 100 learning disabled children to the histories of 200 students who demonstrated satisfactory academic performance. The LPII was filled out on all subjects. Data indicate that the presence of birth and/or developmental abnormalities can be used as a screening instrument. Hoffman finds that 93 percent of the learning disabled subjects have had one or more abnormalities.

Wilborn and Smith (1971) carried out a similar study with a population from a wider range of social, cultural, economic, and ethnic backgrounds. They found 77 percent of their subjects (students who had been referred to the Pupil Appraisal Center of North Texas State University) to have one or more abnormalities as indicated by the LPII.

Wilborn and Smith conclude that the LPII can be used as a screening device not only by physicians but also by school personnel. Schools could request personal and developmental histories on their students and thereby screen large numbers of children with relative ease. Used in conjunction with personal observations, the LPII can be utilized to determine which students appear to warrant further study for specific learning problems

Table 5 will provide a quick review of screening instruments discussed in this chapter.

Table 5 Screening Instruments

Author(s)	Instrument Name	Purpose/Function	Age of Administration	Testing Time	Administrator
Ahr, A. E. (1967)	Screening Test for Academic Readiness (STAR)	Group, pre-school	4-0 to 6-5 years	Less than 1 hour	Teacher
Denhoff, E. Siqueland, M. Komich, M. Hainsworth, P. (1967)	Meeting Street School Screening Test (MSSST) (2 forms)	Identification of cerebral dysfunction or neurological impairment	Kindergarten through Grade 1	Not applicable 20 minutes	Physician Teacher/School Psychologist
Fuller, G. B. Laird, J. T. (1963)	Minnesota Percepto-Diagnostic Test (MPD)	Rapid and objective method for determining whether the etiology of reading disability is organic, primary, secondary	All ages	Less than 1 hour & variable	Teacher/School Psychologists/ Guidance Counselors
Hoffman, M. S. (1971)	Learning Problem Identification Index (LPII)	Physician's identification at earliest possible age of child with low learning potential	Any age	Not applicable	Physician

88

Table 5 *Screening Instruments (continued)*

Author(s)	Instrument Name	Purpose/Function	Age of Administration	Testing Time	Administrator
McLeod, J. (1966)	Dyslexia Schedule (DS)	Assessing aptitude for childhood dyslexia	Grade 1 and any child with reading difficulty	20-25 minutes	Parent (form)
Ozer, M. N. Richardson, H.B. (1972)	Neuro-Developmental Observation (NDO)	Time-limited diagnostic interaction with child to isolate *what works*	5 through 8 years	15 minutes	Physician
Pate, J. E. Webb, W. W. (1966)	First Grade Screening Test (FGST)	Identification of young children with reading problems	Kindergarten	45 minutes	Teacher
Sapir, S. Wilson, B. (1967)	Sapir Development Scale	Identification of learning disabilities at kindergarten level	Kindergarten through 7 years	30 minutes	Trained Kindergarten Teacher
Slingerland, B. H. (1962)	Slingerland Screening Tests for Identifying Children with Specific Language Disability (SST)	Early identification of maturational lag or deficits in the sensory-motor channels	2nd semester of Grade 1 to Grade 4	Varies	Teacher

89

SUMMARY

Currently one of the major areas of concern in learning disabilities is the ability to assess the problem early in order to implement a successful remediation/treatment program. To this end, many screening instruments have been developed during the past few years, and more are likely to be formulated in the future. The individual who seeks to identify and to either remediate or suggest remediation for the learning disability has a host of screening instruments from which to make a choice. The more successful ones have been discussed in this chapter. Discretion should be used by the person employing any specific battery of screening tests.

CHAPTER 7 THE TEACHER AS
A BEHAVIOR RATER

EVIDENCE SHOWING ACCURACY
OF TEACHERS AS EVALUATORS

Traditionally caution has been exercised in using the teacher as a screening agent for predicting the future behavior of students. A much quoted study by Wickman (1928) concludes that teachers' ratings and predictions should be viewed with suspicion. However, a recent trend has developed toward giving greater credence to the opinions of teachers. A study by Henig (1949), with beginning first-grade pupils, and another by Ilg, Ames, and Appel (1965), with young elementary school children, suggest that teachers' evaluations may be useful additions to a predictive index.

Keogh and Smith (1970), in an attempt to identify educationally high-potential and high-risk children, utilized teachers' evaluations on 49 children from kindergarten entrance through grade 5 of a regular school program. Analysis revealed consistently high and significant relationships between teachers' ratings and subsequent school achievement. Teachers were quite accurate in early identification of both high-risk and high-potential children.

Other references supporting teachers as predictors of future behavior of students abound. Keogh and Tchir (1972) found kindergarten and first-grade teachers sensitive to high-risk indicators as reflected in classroom behaviors. Fargo, Roth, and Cade (1968) concluded that preschool teachers are more accurate than pediatricians or psychologists in predicting later school achievement.

Tobiessen, Duckworth, and Conrad (1971) demonstrate the effectiveness of teachers' evaluations using kindergarten rating scales, as do Spivack, Swift, and Prewitt (1971) and Bullock and Brown (1972) for older elementary-age children.

Doehring (1960) illustrates the importance of the classroom observation in the identification of aphasia. Strauss and Lehtinen (1971), as early as 1947, point to the relationship between classroom behavior that is recorded by the teacher and identification of brain-injured children. Bonaker (1967) conducted a study of 1,200 children in 48 kindergarten classes in Johnson City, Kansas. The initial screen consisted of the teachers' choosing one-fourth of their students as high risk in the probability of developing learning problems. Particular emphasis for the teachers was placed upon (1) language development, (2) visual-perceptual adequacy, and (3) fine and gross motor coordination. A standardized battery of tests consisting of the Stanford-Binet and portions of the WISC was then given to those students selected by the teachers. Resulting data confirmed the teacher's key role in the early identification of children with learning disabilities. Although discussion of the accuracy of the identification of children with learning disabilities is premature until the conclusion of the project, Haring and Ridgway (1967) maintain that the individual behavior analysis done by teachers may prove to be a more effective procedure than group testing in identification. The researchers emphasize that learning deficits may be as much a function of the learning environment as they are a function of the organism. This suggests that an adequate basis for preventive and remedial teaching decisions is provided by an ongoing analysis of classroom behavior, with emphasis on the skill, performance, and language-reflected variables as they involve classroom learning tasks.

THE BEHAVIORAL APPROACH

Concurrent with the greater acceptance of the predictions of the classroom teacher has come an adaptation of the behavioral approach for identification of children with learning disabilities. Behavior principles have been applied in formulating behavior rating scales used as screening instruments by teachers.

A behavioral approach to early identification receives support from a number of independent investigators (Cobb, 1972; Fargo, Roth, and Cade, 1968; Haring and Ridgway, 1967; Westman, Rice, and Bermann, 1967).

Forness (1972) observes highly significant differences in school-related behaviors between children referred to an outpatient clinic for possible learning and/or behavior problems and "normal" peers in the same classroom. Differences are noted in attending behavior and in quantity and quality of interaction with the teachers. The capacity of behavioral observation techniques to differentiate between these two groups of children provides support for a method of identifying high-risk children based primarily on direct observation of classroom behavior and analysis of children's problem-solving styles. Forness raises the question that perhaps enthusiasm for standardized test procedures has obscured the importance of other sources of information.

Becker (1971), using a retrospective design, found that third-grade children with learning problems differ from normally achieving third graders on behavior measures obtained at kindergarten, expecially in attention skills and ability to work independently.

Spivack, Swift, and Prewitt (1971) identify 11 factors derived from the Devereux Elementary School Behavior Rating Scale (Spivack and Swift, 1967), including classroom disturbance, impatience, and anxiety, as predictors of school performance.

Lovitt (1971), in describing his proposed method of assessment of children with learning problems, states that "the end product of an evaluation should be to present to the referring agent information that can be immediately transmitted into programming procedures" (p. 10).

Rhode Island Pupil Identification Scale

The Rhode Island Pupil Identification Scale (RIPIS) has been developed for use on kindergarten to grade 2 children as a simple scale focusing on the pupil's classroom behavior (Novack, Bonaventura, and Merenda, 1973). The primary functions of the instrument as stated by its designers are: (1) to help classroom teachers identify children with learning problems, (2) to help classroom teachers indicate readily specific aspects of the school problem requiring attention, and (3) to permit a classroom teacher or specialist to address himself to resolution of a specific school problem as observed in its natural surroundings.

The RIPIS is a 40-item rating scale in which each item is scored according to a Likert Scale. The instrument was standardized on a sample of 851 subjects drawn from seven schools in Rhode Island. Novack et al. categorize the RIPIS as a time-saving device that requires relatively little orientation to its usage and does not take teaching time from the child and the teacher. The scale items lend themselves to operational units rather than to broad-range objectives.

Furthermore, the scale appears to meet the classroom teacher's need for a reporting device that permits her to observe systematically and to indicate behavior considered significant in the presence of various learning activities. There is no need for the specialist to cross the threshold, risking disruption. The instrument can be used as a periodic report to pinpoint aspects of a child's school status to his parents, school psychologist, guidance counselor, school nurse, and family physician.

The uniqueness of this scale rests in its being a multidimensional educational instrument. It permits the educator to make her observations in an educational environment on a child faced with educational tasks and to report educational complaints in educational language.

94

Test Behavior Observation Guide

Attwell, Orpert, and Meyers (1967) report that behaviors as assessed with their Test Behavior Observation Guide are highly related to learning problems in elementary school. Their longitudinal study is concerned with the observations of behavior in kindergarten children as a means of predicting school achievement 5 years later. Behavior ratings completed by teachers were correlated with the California Achievement Test scores of the same subjects when they reached the fifth grade. Attention was found to be an especially powerful predictor. Attwell et al. conclude that the Test Behavior Observation Guide may be a promising device for predicting academic achievement for kindergarten youngsters. Its relative simplicity and evidence of predictability are cited as advantages, though its reliability has yet to be established.

A Behavior Guide (Raskin and Taylor)

Raskin and Taylor (1973) maintain that teachers *are aware of,* and sensitive to, certain behavior patterns or "incident clusters" which have diagnostic significance. The problem teachers face when attempting to report diagnostic information about children is one of organization and description, not lack of expertise. Raskin and Taylor, therefore, have designed a behavior guide as a model for organizing teachers' observations. Behaviors are placed into one of six categories that are critical for the analysis and prediction of academic and/or sociopsychological difficulty: (1) visual behavior—irregular eye movements, eyes too close to paper, poor posture; (2) motor behavior—lack of agility, avoidance of group games, fidgeting; (3) graphics—inaccurate form copying, lack of drawing details; (4) physical condition—poor attendance, small and thin in stature; (5) multi-sensory factors—extreme reliance on more than one sensory mode in simple task, shutting out of multi-sensory information; (6) social-emotional factors—stubborn, bossy, negative, aggressive, destructive, cyclical behavior. Although not specifically stated, the assumption can be made that the behavioral observation model can be used with children of all ages.

Schenectady Kindergarten Rating Scale

Conrad and Tobiessen (1967) have undertaken the development of a rating scale to meet the need for an economical means of screening large numbers of children. The two-pronged working hypothesis of these researchers is: (1) Most children whose behavior and poor achievement will be disturbing to themselves and others during their first 4 years in school can be identified in kindergarten, and (2) the nature of their eventual problems can be predicted from their behavior in kindergarten. Their instrument, the Schenectady Kindergarten Rating Scale (SKRS), defines 14 behavior dimensions (such as waiting and sharing, level of organization of play, clarity of speech, use of materials, and peer relationships) which they found to be significant. The initial stages of the study have shown adequate inter-rater reliability, and several validity studies have been initiated.

Pupil Rating Scale

Myklebust and Boshes (1969) developed the Pupil Rating Scale (PRS) in an extensive study to determine which diagnostic measures best identify children with learning disabilities. The PRS is for normal children between 4 and 8 years old or for retarded children of any age. The child is rated in each of five areas: (1) auditory comprehension and listening, (2) spoken language, (3) orientation, (4) behavior, and (5) motor.

The validity of the PRS was evaluated by comparing two groups of children identified on the basis of test results from that instrument together with reading and WISC vocabulary scores. The learning disabled group scored significantly lower than the other children on each measure. Bryan and McGrady (1972), in their analysis of the PRS, conclude that the instrument is an efficient and economical measure for screening purposes. The teacher is directly involved in the intensive evaluation of a few children. The PRS may identify specific areas of disability despite a child's adequate overall performance. Bryan and McGrady recommend further study of the validity and the basis upon which teachers make discriminations.

Proger (1973), in evaluating the PRS, describes the major advantages of this instrument to be: (1) in administration each child can be screened at a teacher's leisure without disrupting regular class schedule, and (2) indirect observation does not cue a child as to what is happening and so test contamination factors such as sensitization are not critical. Although finding the technical features of the instrument well documented, Proger feels the norms of the PRS are not extensive and that there is almost a total ignoring of reliability. Moreover, the test manual fails to indicate when the PRS should be administered.

SUMMARY

Once the child has started school, there is one person who is in a position to observe the child's reactions to all types of stimuli in all types of situations: the teacher. Why not use this information as a predictive index of high risk and high potential?

Many authors have shown high correlations between teacher's behavior rating scales and other standardized instruments. The advantage of this type of approach is that it permits the teacher to make observations in an educational environment on a child faced with educational tasks and to report educational complaints in educational language. Not only could large numbers of children be screened in a short period of time, but also the results would prove educationally relevant.

CHAPTER 8 TEACHING STRATEGIES

CLASSIFICATIONS OF EDUCATIONAL APPROACHES
Numerous remedial-diagnostic approaches for teaching the learning disabled presently exist. There also is a variety of models for categorizing the respective theoretical orientations. For example, Ysseldyke and Salvia (1974) divide remedial diagnostic approaches into two schools. On one hand, there are those who view the disabled learner as having a dysfunction in an underlying ability that needs to be remedied. The focus in that approach is to assess performance such as neurological, motor, perceptual, or language processes and then to implement remedial strategies designed to ameliorate identified deficits, which would in turn lead to higher-level cognitive learning. On the other hand, members of the second school of thought prefer to directly assess academic and/or behavioral deficits and provide remediation without speculating on underlying causes. This approach is generally referred to as task analysis, an outgrowth of behaviorism; whereas the former approach is considered to be embedded in cognitive psychology (McCarthy, 1976).

Johnson and Morasky (1977) present a model in which they categorize educational approaches according to the aspects of learning that the various theories tend to emphasize. For example, some theorists tend to stress developmental factors. A sequence of development is outlined (perhaps motor, neurological, language, etc.), and the learner receives instruction according to his assumed level of performance within that hierarchy. The five categories within the Johnson and Morasky Model are (1) developmental approaches; (2) basic processes approach; (3) deficit behavior, or task approach; (4) assessment approach; and (5) management approach.

Another method for categorizing educational approaches, the one used in this text, is assigning groups according to the primary areas of remediation and their respective theorists. A direct relationship exists between specific instructional approaches and the professional orientation of their developers. To illustrate, many persons who have worked directly with brain-injured individuals or have based their work on other professionals who did propose that learning disabilities result primarily from some form of cerebral dysfunction. Therefore, in an effort to enable the learner to develop compensating skills for observed deficiencies, the educational model of this orientation stresses perceptual-motor activities, structure, and routine. With other theorists, language development and related skills are emphasized. The position taken in their model is that learning disabilities are rooted in deficit language and sensory systems. Behaviorists, for a final example, place primary emphasis on the stimulus-response process. Individuals subscribing to this orientation suggest that remediation be based largely on observed skill deficiencies, utilizing behavioral techniques in instruction.

Since many of the strategies for teaching learning disabled children are related, only select, representative ones that relate to (1) perceptual-motor processes, (2) language, and (3) task analysis will be reviewed in this chapter. They are the ones considered to have made the greatest impact on the field.

REMEDIATION THROUGH
PERCEPTUAL-MOTOR-BASED PROGRAMS

Kephart's Approach

Newell C. Kephart (1971), in his theory of perceptual-motor development, posits that the individual passes through stages of development characterized by motor performance, perceptual-motor match, perceptual integration, and concept formation. According to Kephart, motor is the earliest and most basic learning upon which are built higher-level perceptual and cognitive skills. During the motor stage the child must develop certain patterns and generalizations of which posture and balance are the most basic. Through the establishment of posture and balance, one is able to respond and move efficiently around her physical environment. Other general motor activities to be developed at this stage are laterality, the awareness within the organism of right and left sides; directionality, the ability to determine right and left outside one's body; and body image, evidenced by the child's ability to identify body parts, control body parts, and correctly position her body in space.

As stated previously, Kephart's theoretical framework makes the assumption that all behavior is based on motor functions. Once the child has acquired these basic motor generalizations, he is then able to explore his environment perceptually and make the perceptual-motor match. Perceptual-motor match requires that the child correlate motor and perceptual information. Examples of such matchings are (1) correctly determining the shape and size of an object when viewing it from different perspectives and (2) using eye-hand coordination in tasks such as writing. Kephart (1971) relates the example of the child who is unable to draw a geometric design because he overemphasizes or equates motor functioning to perceptual performance rather than the reverse. Here, the child concentrates on separate parts of the figure as he draws it, thus obtaining a distorted form. Preferably the child would have a perceptual awareness of the form and match this to previously acquired motor responses. As the child

101

passes through the developmental stages, perceptual (especially visual) skills gain in importance while sensory-motor skills become less significant for obtaining information about one's environment.

The final stage is that of *conceptualization* in which the child develops concepts and generalizations based on previously acquired percepts. Kephart points out that space is very important for this stage of development since "The child who has difficulty with space is likely to have similar difficulties in thinking" (Kephart, 1960, p. 94). This position is based on the belief that objects must be located in space before they can be categorized and thus dealt with in abstraction. Using this theoretical orientation, Kephart (1960, p. 121) developed a training program on the position:

> . . . that many of the children who show difficulty in school learning at grades one to three will also show difficulties in perceptual-motor development and that these perceptual-motor difficulties are related to the problem of school achievement. In such cases the first problem is to identify the point of breakdown. When this point has been discovered, training techniques can be applied which will aid the child in overcoming his difficulty and will permit him to continue his development.

This statement capsulizes Kephart's training program, i.e., the necessity of identifying and assessing developmental stages and providing training where deficiencies exist. It also makes clear why this remediation program stressing skills typically developed by very young children includes many activities found in regular kindergarten or "readiness" classes.

Sensory-motor learning, ocular control, and form perception are the major areas of development on which Kephart focuses in his training program. The stages are considered developmental in that the child should have at least the minimal competencies in sensory-motor and ocular-control areas before receiving training in form perception.

Chalkboard training, which is not considered a major development area but contributes to the acquisition of basic

102

movement patterns, is the first major training presented by Kephart. This category encompasses a variety of activities, progressing sequentially from scribbling, considered to be the prerequisite to copying or drawing; to directionality activities such as "Clock Game" or "Chalkboard Directionality"; through the processes of tracing, copying, and reproducing until the child finally arrives at the point where these activities can be performed on paper rather than the chalkboard.

Sensory-motor training also is sequential in that it first attempts to develop balance and posture through the use of walking and balance boards. Laterality and body image are increased through activities such as "Angels in the Snow" in which the child lies on the floor and moves his limbs according to direction. Rhythm activities such as beating patterns on a drum contribute to laterality as well as perception skills.

Developing eye control is the basis of Kephart's *ocular control training.* This section consists of activities such as ocular pursuit training, which contains stages of training ranging from the child's simply following an object with his eyes to following a ball with his eyes while keeping his hands on the ball. Another activity is the marsden ball in which the child is expected to make various responses, such as touch the ball while it is suspended and moving.

Form perception is the final training category presented by Kephart. In this area Kephart suggests that the child be provided with puzzles, whereby emphasis is placed on the total form rather than simple elements; and stick figures and pegboards, whereby the child is given a model and required to reproduce it. For each of these activities Kephart provides specific directions on how and when the teacher should proceed.

Doman-Delacato Approach
While other motor theories exist, e.g., the movigenic theory of Ray Barsch, which is primarily concerned with the child's movement within space, and the theory of Bryant J. Cratty, who emphasizes the importance of movement activities with learning disabled children (Learner, 1976), the most contro-

versial and divergent motor theory is that of Glenn Doman and Carl Delacato. The theoretical approach as outlined by Delacato (1959) is based on the neurological development and organization of the individual. According to Delacato, the development of the individual (ontogenetics) "recapitulates" the evolution of man (phylogenetics). That is, the development of the individual from conception to adulthood is similar to that of the evolution of the species of man. Neural development is considered to commence during the first trimester of gestation and continues until about 8 years of age, when one hemisphere of the brain becomes dominant as evidenced by the establishment of handedness. The development of the individual is related as follows:

1. Medulla and Spinal Cord. From gestation through about 16 weeks all actions are reflex in nature, some of which provide for survival.

2. Pons Level. To about 6 months of age visual and auditory senses gain in importance and the infant begins crawling.

3. Midbrain Level. Ten months of age. Child begins cross-pattern creeping and acquires mobility with greater efficiency and smoothness.

4. Early Cortex Level. One year of age. Child begins cross-pattern walking which is smooth and rhythmical.

5. Cortical Hemispheric Dominance. Eight years of age. Hemispheric dominance has been established. "Sidedness" is evident.

Failure to follow this sequence, according to Delacato (1963), will result in communication problems such as aphasia, delayed speech, stuttering, retarded reading, poor spelling and handwriting; also reading which falls in the normal range, but is below mathematical performance. In the Doman-Delacato program, children evidencing learning disabilities are assessed according to this hierarchy to determine the lowest stage of dysfunction. A significant factor in the program is that it is geared toward complete neurological organization. Although other programs prescribe treatment along a developmental sequence, only the Doman-Delacato approach advocates complete neurological organization. Specifically, the aims are that the treatment procedures will remediate the dysfunctions of the brain rather than simply correct the corresponding motor, perceptual, and cognitive functions. The remediation program is outlined as follows:

1. Medulla and Spinal Cord. Child is placed on floor and engages in reflex movements for most of waking hours.
2. Pons Level. Child is taught to crawl, and given vision training in order to help him become bi-ocular.
3. Midbrain Level. Child receives training for pattern creeping, visual pursuit of a moving target, for tonal memory and auditory discrimination through listening to recordings and for bilaterality through large ball games.
4. Early Cortical Level. Training includes mastery of cross-pattern walking and visual fusion exercises using large muscle activities with emphasis on the trampoline.
5. Cortical Hemispheric Dominance. Music activities are completely eliminated from child's life. "Sidedness" is developed by altering sleeping patterns and forcing the child to engage in activities using only the dominant side. A classroom remedial reading program consisting of learning words by the whole context, by structural analysis, and by phonetic analysis is also provided.

Hallahan and Kauffman (1976, p. 136) state that the criticism of this highly controversial treatment program has primarily centered on the following: "(1) The promotional methods place parents in an uneasy position if they refuse the treatment. (2) The regimens are so demanding that the parents may neglect other family needs and the child may be inhibited from engaging in normal age appropriate activities. (3) Their claims of success are exaggerated and undocumented. (4) The theoretical underpinnings of their practices are weak."

Frostig's Approach

Perception is generally defined as the process of receiving, integrating, and interpreting environmental stimuli (Kephart, 1975). Attempting to distinguish perception from lower-order functioning (such as acuity) and higher-order cognition involving thinking and meaningful language, Hammill (1975) describes perceptual processes as " . . . those brain operations that involve interpreting and organizing the physical elements of the stimulus rather than the symbolic aspects of the stimulus" (p. 204). In the classroom children evidencing difficulties in tracing, copying, reversals, discriminating figures, etc., may be considered to have perceptual handicaps. More specifically, these difficulties would be defined as visual perceptual handicaps. Marianne Frostig (1976), basing her work on the pioneering efforts of professionals such as Alfred Strauss, Laura Lehtinen, Newell Kephart, Maria Montessori, William Cruickshank, and others, developed an assessment instrument (Developmental Test of Visual Perception) and training program for visual perception. As a result of her work with children, Frostig was convinced that visual perceptual abilities were crucial for overall school success. Frostig (Frostig and Maslow, 1973; Frostig, 1976) identified five subskills of visual perception and related training activities: figure-ground perception, visual-motor coordination, perceptual constancy, position in space, and spatial relations.

1. *Figure-Ground Perception.* Refers to child's ability to identify the most salient items in a stimulus field and tune out the irrelevant. For example, an affected child might have difficulties finding hidden figures in a puzzle, locating a word in a dictionary, or paying attention. Suggested activities might include pointing out stimuli in everyday activities ("Do you see the little bird in the grass?"), sorting or discriminating activities such as finding sets of red things.

2. *Visual-Motor Coordination.* Refers to a child's ability to coordinate vision with various body movements. For example, an affected child has difficulties in copying from chalkboard, coloring within lines, tracing, writing, pasting, finger tracing, doing finger games, handling manipulative toys, stringing beads, and doing self-help activities.

3. *Perceptual Constancy.* Refers to ability to recognize a

form regardless of stimulus conditions. For example, child does not recognize geometric shape such as circle when colored differently. Suggested activities include learning names of planes (circle, square, triangle, etc.) and solids (sphere, cube, cone, etc.), recognizing pictures of planes and solids, and finding and sorting items according to shape and size.

4. *Position in Space.* Refers to ability to consistently perceive the direction of a stimulus item. For example, the child reverses b and d. Suggested activities include exercises where children position bodies in relation to objects (climb *on* a chair), exercises with left and right, and reversing/rotating geometric shapes.

5. *Spatial Relationships.* Refers to ability to perceive relationships among symbols as well as to oneself. The affected child has difficulty in copying, working with material with too many items on a page, multiplication and division. Suggested activities include emphasizing three-dimensional objects, placing blocks according to position (on, over, under, over, etc.), reproducing patterns using pegs, blocks, marbles, etc., and doing paper and pencil exercises.

Despite the fact that the Frostig Developmental Test of Visual Perception has been employed widely and frequently indiscriminately in instructional programs (Smith and Marx, 1972), factor analytic studies indicate that this scale probably only assesses two, rather than five, factors related to motor and "perceptual organization" (Smith and Marx, 1972; Zach and Kaufman, 1972). Although Frostig contends that perceptual training as outlined in her program facilitates initial reading, Smith and Marx (1972) conclude, "Whatever the DTVP measures, it is not reading ability, and caution should be exercised in using it as a screening instrument to predict future achievement or as a device to diagnose specific perceptual variables underlying reading deficiency" (p. 361). Additional experimental evidence relative to the low reliability/validity of such instruments and the limited efficacy of related training programs has been reported in the literature (Bortner, 1974; Ysseldyke and Salvia, 1974; Hammill, 1975).

Validity of Perceptual-Motor Training Programs

Considering the absence of empirical evidence that: (1) existing instruments actually assess discrete perceptual abilities or that (2) training in the related subskills enhances higher-level cognitive functioning, the conclusions of the various reviewers are probably warranted. That is, except in the rare cases where the goal is the training of specific perceptual skills per se, perceptual-motor training programs are unwarranted and possibly inefficient, especially when considering the exorbitant financial costs and teaching time these programs demand. This conclusion is further supported by the works of Quay (1973), Ysseldyke and Salvia (1974), and Hammill (1975).

REMEDIATION THROUGH LANGUAGE-BASED PROGRAMS

Johnson—Myklebust Model

Another major approach to learning disabilities has been in the area of auditory learning and language. Johnson and Myklebust (1967) have developed a psychoneurological model of learning disabilities which considers: intraneurosensory learning, interneurosensory learning, and integrative learning. This model is based on the theoretical concept that the ". . . brain is made up of semi-independent systems, and that at times a given system, such as auditory or visual system, functions semi-independently from others. At times one system functions in a supplementary way with another, and at times all systems function interrelatedly" (Johnson, 1969, p. 80). Intraneurosensory learning refers to learning which involves only one sensory system such as auditory discrimination or auditory memory. Interneurosensory learning involves converting or "transducing" from one system to another such as taking a visual symbol and making an auditory association. Specifically, it occurs when the child looks at the letter *b* and

108

is required to make the *b* sound. Integrative learning requires that all systems function as a unit. Here one must translate experiences into symbols for purposes such as thinking. Integrative learning is exemplified when the child is required to comprehend what he reads. Johnson and Myklebust (1967) also propose the concept of overloading in which a child may have difficulty processing information through more than one system at a time. For example, a child may experience learning difficulties if he must utilize auditory, visual, and motor systems simultaneously.

According to this model, if psychoneurological disturbances occur, i.e., dysfunction within the semi-independent systems, learning disorders result.

Hierarchy of Learning Disabilities Johnson and Myklebust (1967) specify a hierarchy of learning disabilities, indicating a developmental component as follows:

Sensation Refers to the performance of the sensory organs. It is the lowest level behavior. Dysfunctions are manifested in the form of blindness or deafness.

Perception Refers to the proper reception and interpretation of environmental stimuli. Its importance in the developmental sequence resides in the fact that it is considered to affect higher-level experiences.

Imagery Refers to the ability of the individual to accurately, visually and auditorially recall perceptual experiences. Memory assumes major importance.

Symbolization Refers to proficiency in both verbal (language) and nonverbal (judgment in measurements such as time, distance, size, etc.) behaviors. Within this category is provided a sequence of language development, consisting of inner language, receptive language, and expressive language.

The category of symbolization is further broken down into inner language, receptive language, and expressive language. A brief description of these subcategories follows.

1. *Inner Language.* The first phase of language to develop. Inner language evidences itself in the child's ability to make proper associations regarding environmental ob-

jects, such as properly arranging doll furniture. The child who fails to associate bark with dog may be experiencing an inner language disorder.

2. *Receptive Language.* Refers to a stage beginning at approximately 8 months of age when the child starts to respond to command and his name. It is a building upon inner language. Children with receptive language disorders have difficulty understanding what is being said to them. While the disorder exists in varying degrees of severity, children suffering from it may not understand basic words, such as walk, or more abstract words, such as *on* and *under,* or complex sentences, such as "Before you sit down, close the door." Treatment for this disorder should begin early, at 3 or 4 years of age, if necessary. Training involves breaking the language down into small meaningful units, providing sufficient repetition, and making sure that the child has the personal experiences to associate with the word. Through experiences parts of speech are taught, beginning with nouns and proceeding with verbs, prepositions, adjectives, adverbs, and pronouns. For example, when teaching the word run, one engages the child in running activities.

3. *Expressive Language.* Refers to a stage based upon the acquisition of inner and receptive language. Expressive language emerges at about one year of age. Johnson and Myklebust (1967) further subcategorize expressive language difficulties into reauditorization, apraxia, and defective syntax. A brief description of these subcategories follows.

   a. *Reauditorization.* Difficulty in retrieving words even though the meaning of the word is known. Children manifesting this disorder will frequently substitute words such as pie for cake or use gestures to express themselves. Training should stress meaningful activities, helping children organize information, facilitating recall, drill, self-monitoring, and practice. For example, to facilitate recall, Johnson and Myklebust (1967) suggest the presentation of incomplete sentences/phrases where children are required to supply the missing word, e.g., "bread and _____ " or "I sleep in a _____ " (p. 119). Other activities might include presenting a series of pictures of common objects for this student to name rapidly or having the student touch the object to recall its name.

b. *Apraxia.* Difficulty in making the motor responses necessary for achieving desired sounds. Instruction focuses on teaching the child how to make the corresponding motor and sound responses. Techniques may involve the teacher demonstrating for the child to imitate, or the teacher instructing the child how to position tongue and lips, or the teacher manipulating the child's tongue, lips, and jaw to make the desired sounds.

c. *Defective Syntax.* Difficulty organizing words into complete sentences. Children in this group may have difficulty with adjective-noun phrases, with the noun-verb-object sequence, etc. In instructing the child, the teacher provides "structured" sentences which are properly paired with the corresponding experiences. An illustration of such might be where one initially teaches the child to use the noun-verb-object sequence such as "Mommy is eating" by engaging the child in the activity and using nouns (mommy) that are familiar to the child. Once this sequence is learned, the object is introduced, such as "Mommy is eating soup." (p. 138), while pictures of this activity are simultaneously presented. Gradually the teacher omits words for the child to insert until the child is saying the entire sentence independently. Johnson and Myklebust point out that this language training is similar to that provided in foreign language instruction.

Conceptualization Refers to the ability to engage in abstractions and to categorize. It is the highest level process in the Johnson and Myklebust hierarchy. Deficits in any of the lower-level processes, i.e., perception, imagery, or symbolization, are considered to interfere with conceptualization skills. For example, Johnson and Myklebust point out that children with deficits in spontaneous language usage would have difficulty formulating concepts.

Remediation within the Model Remediation within the Johnson-Myklebust (1967) Model involves (1) an analysis of the child's psychoneurological learning systems (intraneurosensory, interneurosensory, and integrative), (2) specification of type of learning disability within the learning sequence (perception, imagery, symbolization, or conceptualization), and the identification of particular deficit skill areas such as reading, writing, auditory language, or math. This educational planning can be seen in the approach to the auditory or visual dyslexic in reading (Johnson, 1969).

After it is determined that the learner is a "visual dyslexic" (while auditory learning is intact) as indicated by reversals of letters and failure to remember whole words, initial instruction primarily utilizes a phonics approach. The child is taught to blend consonants and short vowels into words. After acquiring a substantial reading vocabulary, the child receives training to develop visual skills by emphasizing the visual aspects of known words. On the other hand, the auditory dyslexic who has difficulties making finer discriminations between sounds is taught initially by a sight approach. Without the adult's orally naming the words (in order to avoid interference from another mode), the child is instructed to match whole words with pictures depicting their meaning. After developing a sufficient sight vocabulary, the child receives auditory training utilizing techniques such as intensifying the auditory stimulus or highlighting visual similarities for particular sounds.

Although Johnson and Myklebust identify several types of learning disabilities, disorders of auditory language are considered to be the most severe, and performance in other academic areas are somewhat dependent upon its remediation. Other aspects of their remediation model include per-

112

ceptual training, multisensory instruction, readiness levels, and nonverbal areas of experience. The overriding consideration is that regardless of technique, the instructional program must be tailored to the individual child (Johnson and Myklebust, 1967, and Myklebust, 1975).

Kirk-McCarthy-Kirk Model

Another major approach to language and learning disabilities has been provided by Kirk, McCarthy, and Kirk (Kirk, 1976) in the development of the Illinois Test of Psycholinguistic Abilities (ITPA) (Kirk and McCarthy, 1968). The ITPA was designed to analyze psycholinguistic abilities so that remediation and training could follow (Kirk, 1975). Psycholinguistics is an attempt to study the mental processes which determine language acquisition and use, i.e., the psychology of language structure (Newcomer and Hammill, 1976).

Organizing Processes Incorporating Osgood's (1953) model of communication, the ITPA includes *psycholinguistic process, levels of organization,* and a third dimension not considered by Osgood, *channels of communication.* The focus of the ITPA, as with the Osgood model, is to determine the organizing processes within the brain during the stimulus-response sequence. That is, once the stimulus occurs, what associations take place within the brain that result in the observed responses? This model suggests that the mediating processes are based upon previously learned information which is used in the formulation of generalizations. The assumption is that within normal learning, certain prescribed associations and responses will occur. To illustrate, when presented the auditory stimulus, "Bread is to eat, milk is to _____ " (Newcomer and Hammill, 1976, p. 25), the child will make associations with previous experiences and respond "drink."

The three psycholinguistic processes are: (1) receptive process (input), (2) organizing process (internal relating of what is received) and (3) expressive processes (output). The receptive processes which assess whether or not the child understands the external stimuli include auditory and visual reception. The organizing processes which make assumptions relative to how stimuli are internally organized include auditory and visual associations. Verbal and manual expression are the operations incorporated within the category of expressive processes—the type of responses used to convey ideas.

In addition to having these classifications according to stimuli processing, the ITPA also is categorized according to the level of information processing, i.e., the representational level and the automatic level. The representational level (the higher level) requires symbolic associations involving semantics, abstractions, problem solving, etc.

ITPA Subtests The ITPA subtests and their descriptions are as follows:

Auditory Reception Ability to derive meaning from speech. The child is required to answer questions such as "Do ponies fly? "

Visual Reception Ability to derive meaning from visual symbols. The child is presented a picture (trash can) which is removed; a set of four pictures is then presented, and the child is directed to find a similar one (wastebasket).

Auditory Association Ability to make generalizations from auditory symbols. The child must associate as in "A rabbit is fast; a turtle is _____ ."

Visual Association Ability to make generalizations from visual symbols. The child must, for example, match a picture of cheese with a picture of a rat.

Verbal Expression Ability to express verbally. The child is required to express a variety of concepts about familiar objects.

Manual Expression Child uses movement or pantomime to express variety of ideas about familiar objects. The automatic level is the lower level which involves less voluntary, nonmeaningful behaviors. Tasks at this level do not require the degree of "conceptual mediation" required at the representational level.

114

Grammatic Closure Ability to use grammar automatically, e.g., "Here is a bed; here are two _____ ."

Auditory Closure (Supplementary Test) Ability to complete incomplete word given orally, e.g., tele/one and bo/le.

Sound Blending (Supplementary Test) Ability to blend into complete word phonetic sounds given orally, e.g., c-u-p and b-o-a-t.

Visual Closure Ability to identify visual stimulus from incomplete representation, e.g., child identifies partially pictured dogs.

Auditory Sequential Memory Ability to recall varying (2 to 8) sequences of digits given by the examiner.

Visual Sequential Memory Ability to recall and reproduce series of nonmeaningful visual symbols.

Channels of Communication Finally, the Kirk et al. model considers channels of communication, specifically the auditory-vocal and the visual-motor channels. As reported by Newcomer and Hammill (1976, p. 22), these models were arbitrarily selected by the authors ". . . since they felt these particular sensory pathways were the most critical for learning." The channels of communication specify the sensory modes by which the child will receive and respond to information. A simplistic schematic presentation of the ITPA is shown in Table 6.

Administration of the ITPA yields an "intraindividual" profile, depicting strengths and deficiencies among the various subtests. Remedial suggestions include (1) training in areas where deficiencies are indicated, (2) utilizing areas of strength for instruction, and (3) using multisensory approaches.

Programs Based on ITPA Rather extensive remedial programs based on the ITPA have been developed by Minskoff, Wiseman, and Minskoff—MWM Program for Developing Language Abilities (1972). The MWM program contains teaching activities which correspond directly to the 12 subtests of the ITPA. Instructional tasks involve a series of activities de-

115

Table 6   Schematic Presentation of the ITPA

	Receptive Processes	Organizing Processes	Expressive Processes
Representational Level	Auditory Reception	Auditory Association	Verbal Expression
	Visual Reception	Visual Association	Manual Expression
Automatic Level		Auditory Closure	
		Auditory Sequential Memory	
		Visual Closure	
		Visual Sequential Memory	

signed to remediate deficiencies as indicated by the ITPA assessment data. For example, on the ITPA subtest in auditory reception (Kirk and McCarthy, 1968) the child is required to answer questions such as "Do airplanes fly? " A simple teaching activity as suggested in the MWM program would be to say the word "car" in conjunction with presenting pictures of cars (Newcomer and Hammill, 1976).

Bush and Giles (1969) have also developed a series of teaching activities which correspond to the subtests of the ITPA. These activities are organized according to elementary grade levels (1-6) and general techniques such as following directions or identifying objects. Continuing the above auditory reception example, teaching activities suggested by Bush and Giles (1969, p. 4) for auditory reception at grade one include solving riddles such as "What do cats like to chase?" or "What hides its face with its hands?"

Validity of Language-Based Programs

Although language programs based in part on the ITPA have been widely accepted and utilized, evaluations have been similar to those of the perceptual-motor programs, i.e., there is little or no empirical evidence attesting to the validity (Ysseldyke and Salvia, 1974; Hallahan and Kauffman, 1976) and efficacy of related training (Newcomer and Hammill, 1976). However, Kirk (1976) points out that the effectiveness of the ITPA has been somewhat clouded in that it has been overused, misused, and misperceived.

REMEDIATION THROUGH TASK-ANALYTIC-BASED PROGRAMS

Focus of Task Analysis

Placing primary emphasis on the task rather than on the learner is the focus of the task-analytic approach. Task analysis is a procedure designed to enable teachers to become more skilled in executing goal-directed instruction. The process involves the identification and sequentialization of skills located in criterion-referenced systems, the identification and sequentialization of prerequisite subskills of the terminal behavior, and the systematic instruction of these skills. Johnson and Morasky (1977) list five reasons for the task analysis:

1. To identify sequential skills used to determine skill deficiencies. Hierarchy is used as assessment tool, determining whether or not child is able to perform task.
2. To determine proper skills, decisions, discriminations, etc., to be taught once discrepancy has been identified. Teacher specifies each aspect of skill required in task performance.
3. To determine prerequisite skills child must have prior to instruction.
4. To indicate the obvious instructional sequence. The composite terminal skill is broken down into its components and sequenced.

Basic Features of Task Analysis

The first step in task analysis is skill identification. "What

117

specific educational tasks are important for the child to learn?" (Learner, 1976, p. 110). Skills taught in the classroom are typically those taken from curriculum guides and commercial materials (Myers and Hammill, 1969; Stephens, 1977). However, as Myers and Hammill point out, these sources are generally ineffective for learning disabled children since the skills are not listed discretely or sequentially. In skill oriented task analytic systems such as the one developed by Stephens (1977), discrete empirical skills are identified from traditional sources and then listed according to scope and sequence. For example, reading is divided into major categories such as phonetic analysis, structural analysis, comprehension, and so forth. The major categories then are broken down into subcategories, such as punctuation and syllabication within the major category of structural analysis. The skills, stated operationally, are listed within the categories and subcategories according to grade level. Presented schematically, one category and subcategory would appear as in Table 7.

As can be seen in Table 7, the scope is presented along the horizontal axis while the sequence falls along the vertical axis. Students are individually evaluated on assessment tasks designed for each skill. In the Level 3 punctuation skill, the student would be given an unpunctuated paragraph and directed to supply the punctuation. The assessment process continues in this manner with the examiner recording unmastered skills.

Once skill deficiencies have been determined, the next step is to analyze the objective in terms of the learner. The second question then becomes, "What does the learner need to be able to do before he can perform this task? " (Popham and Baker, 1970, p. 68). This is referred to as identifying entry or prerequisite behaviors. Notice the procedure for the following objective: When presented with a letter and set of two additional letters, the student will identify the letter in the set that is the same as the one initially presented. The learner must: (1) have a basic understanding of what is meant by the terms like and different; (2) be able to visually dis-

118

Table 7 Sample Scope and Sequence of Punctuation Subcategory

Major Category:

Subcategories	Upper & Lower Case Letters	Punctuation	Structural Analysis			
			Singular & Plural Word Endings	Word Building	Compound Words	Prefix/Suffix
Level 0 skills						
Level 1 skills		The student will name punctuation marks.				
Level 2 skills		The student will explain what punctuation marks mean.				
Level 3 skills		The student will use punctuation marks in paragraph.				

From *Teaching skills to children with learning and behavioral disorders* by T. M. Stephens. Columbus, OH: Charles E. Merrill Publishing Co., 1977. Used with permission.

criminate letters; and (3) understand the requirements of the task. After identifying the components of particular skills, one must determine which skills the learner already possesses, which ones must be taught, and what is the most effective method for teaching them. If the child has demonstrated an understanding of the terms like and different, only a review is necessary and one can proceed with succeeding subskills, i.e., visual discrimination and task performance. On the other hand, if the child has not mastered this basic understanding, rather extensive teaching activities may be necessary to develop the conceptual subskill of likeness and differences prior to its use in the composite skill of matching like letters.

The theoretical foundation of task analysis, i.e., breaking subject matter into small steps, organizing it into a logical sequence, building each step upon the preceding one, etc., is based on the operant principles of Skinner (1968). The procedures for developing related instructional sequences also evolve from programming techniques (Johnson and Morasky, 1977).

When teaching a new behavior, one must arrange conditions so that the learner will emit the desired response. Such conditions may take the form of modeling, prompting, shaping, etc. (Skinner, 1968). Skinner also suggests that when modeling, the teacher respond slowly, possibly with exaggerated behavior. The point here is that teachers often incorrectly assume that students have certain rudimentary skills in their repertoire. Another consideration is that students not be asked to do what has not been taught. In teaching letter discrimination, one says, "This is the letter g and here is another just like it; it is also a g." (Teacher demonstrates matching two g's.) As the sequence progresses, prompts should be used, in diminishing degrees, to assure continued accurate responding.

An additional value of prompting is in the high level of responding that results. The importance of student responding has been recognized in frequency (Skinner, 1968; Johnson and Morasky, 1977) and type (Hallahan and Kauffman, 1976). Skinner maintains that ". . . a student does not pas-

120

sively absorb knowledge from the world around him but must play an active role . . . ." (p. 5). Johnson and Morasky (1977) state this as a principle: "In any instructional sequence the student must be called upon to make regularly scheduled, active responses relating to the task" (p. 323). Skinner also stresses the importance of making responses other than oral ones. The facilitative effects of motor responses to academic tasks on the subsequent acquisition of those skills has been demonstrated empirically (Hallahan and Kauffman, 1976).

Popham and Baker (1970) also point out the need for the teacher to allow the student to make the responses he will be evaluated on. They distinguish between equivalent practice, in which the activity requires the exact responses as specified in the terminal behavior, and analogous practice, in which the activity is similar, but not identical, to the terminal behavior. For the learning disabled this distinction is critical since frequently these students become lost in the mechanics of the task rather than performance of the skill per se. For example, in teaching matching letters, the terminal behavior is to have students *circle* the same letter; a child who doesn't quite understand the directions may perform this incorrectly if previously he was permitted only to *point* to the same letter.

Finally, built into the task-analytic approach to instruction are the concepts of evaluation and modification (Johnson and Morasky, 1977; Stephens, 1977). Each teaching strategy should contain an evaluation activity whereby the teacher can determine if the skill has been mastered. The evaluation should reflect the behavioral objective and directly assess its stated skill. For example, if the objective states, "When presented a letter and set of two additional letters, the student will identify the letter in the set that is the same as the one initially presented," the evaluation activity must require that the learner perform this task. If mastery is not reached, additional instruction is needed. When providing additional instruction on the same skill, the teacher must consider how to modify the previous instruction, i.e., whether to further break down the skill, to increase pupil responses, to provide additional practice, or to increase the incentives provided for student performance. It is obvious that strategy modification involves the analysis of two factors: the task and student performance. When modifying the teaching strategy, the teacher should try to vary as few factors as possible while holding others constant.

Validity of Task Analysis

Similar to the approaches stressing learner abilities, the skill training model also has been viewed skeptically (Learner, 1976). In lieu of experimental evidence, its critics question the efficacy of sequential skills in teaching learning disabled children, suggesting that other methods may be more valuable for some children.

SUMMARY

While there are various ways to classify educational approaches to learning disabilities, the classifications used in this text were according to perceptual-motor, language, and task-analytic programs. In the perceptual-motor model emphasis is placed on the identification and training of deficit motor and/or perceptual skills which are considered to lead to higher-level cognitive functioning. Language theorists suggest that learning disabilities may be rooted in underlying linguistic dysfunctions. Particular attention is given to how the learner processes information and how that data can be used for instruction. Task analysis, on the other hand, stresses the skill to be taught. The skill is analyzed and broken down into small sequential steps so that it can be mastered by the learner.

While the theoretical orientations differ, as McCarthy (1976) points out, these approaches may not be mutually exclusive; however, there is a need to find the most efficacious method for teaching these children. To date, the research on educational approaches is not conclusive. Not only has one approach not been demonstrated to be superior, but also there is sufficient reason to question the validity of several models. This observation would suggest that special educators must continue to vigorously research instructional strategies for learning disabled children.

What is apparent from the available literature is that not all children labeled learning disabled would benefit from the same approach. One is naturally led to the conclusion that educators of learning disabled children, in addition to pursuing relevant research, must become (1) keenly aware of the purposes and values of the respective approaches and (2) highly skilled in matching the approach to the child.

CURRENT EDITIONS OF TESTS

This is a list of current editions of tests commercially available. In some cases, older versions of the tests are referenced in text discussion.

Assessment of children's language comprehension. C. R. Foster, J. J. Giddan, and J. Stark. Palo Alto, Calif.: Consulting Psychologists Press, 1972.

Beery-Buktenica developmental test of visual-motor integration. K. E. Beery and N. A. Buktenica. Chicago: Follett Publishing Co., 1967.

Bender visual-motor gestalt test. L. Bender. New York: American Orthopsychiatric Association, 1938.

Boston diagnostic aphasia exam. H. Goodglass and E. Kaplan. Philadelphia: Lea and Febiger, 1972.

California achievement tests. E. W. Tiegs and W. W. Clark. Monterey, Calif.: California Test Bureau, 1970.

Carrow elicited language inventory. E. Carrow. Austin, Tex.: Learning Concepts, 1974.

Developmental sentence scoring. L. Lee. Evanston, Ill.: Northwestern University Press, 1974.

Durrell analysis of reading difficulty. D. D. Durrell. New York: Harcourt, Brace and World, 1955.

Engleman basic concepts inventory. S. Engleman. Chicago: Follett Educational Corporation, 1967.

First grade screening test. J. E. Pate and W. W. Webb. Circle Pines, Minn.: American Guidance Service, Inc., 1966.

Frostig developmental test of visual perception. M. Frostig. Palo Alto, Calif.: Consulting Psychologists Press, 1966.

Gates-MacGinitie reading test. A. I. Gates and W. H. MacGinitie. New York: Teachers College, Columbia University, 1972.

Gates-McKillop reading diagnostic tests. A. I. Gates and A. S. McKillop. Los Angeles: Western Psychological Services, 1962.

Goldman-Fristoe-Woodcock test of auditory discrimination. R. Goldman, M. Fristoe, and R. Woodcock. Circle Pines, Minn.: American Guidance Service, Inc., 1970.

Goodenough draw-a-man test. See *Measurement of intelligence by drawings.*

Goodenough-Harris drawing test. D. B. Harris. Los Angeles: Western Psychological Services, 1963.

Gray oral reading test. H. M. Robinson and A. I. Gray. Los Angeles: Western Psychological Services, 1967.

Harris test of lateral dominance. A. J. Harris. New York: The Psychological Corporation, 1947.

Illinois test of psycholinguistic abilities. S. A. Kirk and J. J. McCarthy. Los Angeles: Western Psychological Services, 1968.

Lincoln-Osertsky motor development scale. W. Sloan. Los Angeles: Western Psychological Services, 1954.

Measurement of intelligence by drawings. F. L. Goodenough. Yonkers-on-Hudson, N.Y.: World Book Co., 1926.

Meeting street school screening test. P. K. Hainsworth and M. L. Siqueland. Providence, R.I.: Crippled Children and Adults of Rhode Island, 1969.

Memory-for-designs. F. K. Graham and D. C. Kendall. Missoula, Mont.: Psychological Test Specialists, 1960.

126

Metropolitan achievement tests. W. N. Durost, H. H. Bixler, J. W. Wrightstone, G. A. Prescot, and I. H. Balow. New York: Harcourt, Brace and World, 1958.

Northwestern syntax screening test: Reception. Evanston, Ill.: Northwestern University Press, 1971.

Otis quick-scoring mental ability test. A. S. Otis. Los Angeles: Western Psychological Services, 1967.

Peabody picture vocabulary test. L. M. Dunn. Circle Pines, Minn.: American Guidance Service, Inc., 1965.

Picture story language test. H. R. Myklebust. Los Angeles: Western Psychological Services, 1965.

Porch index of communicative ability in children. B. Porch. Palo Alto, Calif.: Consulting Psychologists Press, 1974.

Purdue perceptual-motor survey. E. G. Roach and N. C. Kephart. Columbus, Ohio: Charles E. Merrill, 1966.

Raven's progressive matrices test. J. C. Raven. Los Angeles: Western Psychological Services, 1965.

Slosson intelligence test. R. L. Slosson. East Aurora, N.Y.: Slosson Educational Publications, Inc., 1963.

Stanford achievement test. R. Madden, E. F. Gardner, H. C. Rudman, B. Karlsen, and J. C. Merwin. New York: Harcourt, Brace Jovanovich, 1973.

Stanford-Binet intelligence scale. L. M. Terman and M. A. Merrill. Boston: Houghton Mifflin Co., 1973.

Stanford diagnostic reading test. B. Karlsen, R. Madden and E. F. Gardner. New York: Harcourt, Brace and World, 1966.

Templin-Darley tests of articulation. M. C. Templin and F. L. Darley. Iowa City: University of Iowa, Bureau of Educational Research and Service Extension Division, 1969.

Templin picture sound discrimination test. M. Templin. Minneapolis: University of Minnesota Press, 1957.

Test for auditory comprehension of language. E. Carrow. Austin, Tex.: Urban Research Group, 1973.

Vocabulary comprehension scale. T. Bangs. Austin, Tex.: Learning Concepts, 1975.

Wechsler intelligence scale for children. D. Wechsler. New York: The Psychological Corporation, 1974.

Wepman auditory discrimination test. J. M. Wepman. Los Angeles: Western Psychological Services, 1973.

Wide range achievement test. J. F. Jastak and S. R. Jastak. Los Angeles: Western Psychological Services, 1965.

GLOSSARY

Aphasia. Communication disability, a defect or loss of power to express speech, writing, or signs, as well as the inability to comprehend language.

Apraxia. Difficulty in making the motor responses necessary for achieving the desired sounds.

Auditory association. Ability to make generalizations from auditory symbols.

Auditory reception. Ability to derive meaning from speech.

Auditory sequential memory. Ability to recall varying sequences (2 to 8) of digits given orally.

Body image. Ability to identify body parts, control body parts, and correctly position one's body in space.

Coarticulation. Muscle coordination involved in the process producing aspects of sounds in sequence, physically articulated simultaneously.

Conceptualization. Ability to develop concepts and generalizations based on previously acquired percepts.

Constitutional dyslexia. Fairly deep-seated inability to correctly orient written symbols.

Culturally deprived. Reduced sensory stimulation resulting from narrow cultural background.

Defective syntax. Difficulty organizing words into complete sentences.

Directionality. Ability to determine right and left outside one's body.

Dysgraphia. Inability to write.

Dyslexia. See constitutional dyslexia.

Dysphasia. Impairment of speech.

Electroencephalogram (EEG). The method by which electrical discharges from the brain are recorded.

Environmental etiology. Problem of learning caused by inappropriate and detrimental surroundings and stimuli.

Exceptional children. Children unlike normal children; may include the blind, deaf, learning disabled, gifted, emotionally disturbed, etc.

Figure-ground perception. Ability to identify the most salient items in a stimulus field and tune out the irrelevant.

Grammatic closure. Automatic use of grammar.

Gustatory. Referring to taste.

Halo effect. Biasing of test results by giving subject too much information to solve a problem or by counting a half correct answer as totally correct.

Hyperactive. Overactive, hyperkinetic.

Intraneurosensory learning. Learning which involves only one sensory system, such as auditory discrimination or auditory memory.

Kinesthetic. Pertaining to the perception of motion, position, weight, and force of the muscles and body parts.

Laterality. Awareness within the individual of left and right sides.

Lexical. Single-word vocabulary at a preschool level.

Likert scale. Attitude measurement technique; an attitudinal statement followed by a five-response continuum from which the subject selects category that best describes his reaction to the statement.

Longitudinal study. Study of the same population at

different times in their life.

Manual expressions. Use of movement or pantomime to express variety of ideas about familiar objects.

Minimal brain dysfunction. Learning disorder caused by brain damage or biochemical imbalance, a vague term implying only a small affected area; synonyms: minimal brain damage, minimal cerebral injury, minimal cerebral dysfunction.

Neupallium. Section of the brain cortex.

Neurological signs. Outward signs or behaviors indicating some neural impairment.

Olfactory. Referring to the sense of smell.

Organic etiology. Cause of a learning disability which has been demonstrated or inferred to be due to some malfunction of the brain.

Peraption. Process of receiving, integrating, and interpreting environmental stimuli.

Perception. World as it seems to be by evaluation of sensory stimuli.

Perceptual constancy. Ability to coordinate vision with various body movements.

Perceptual motor experience. Process of exposure and motor evaluation of sensory stimuli.

Phonemes. Phonetically similar but slightly different sounds in a language, e.g., the *t* in top, atop, and cat.

Position in space. Ability to consistently perceive the direction of a stimulus item.

Protocol. A standardized test booklet for recording the results of a test.

Psychodynamics. Science of motives and causes of mental processes.

Psycholingenetics. Study of the mental processes which determine language acquisition.

Reauditorization. Difficulty in retrieving words even though the meaning of the word is known.

Reliability. Referring to a testing instrument's ability to always produce the same results when given under the same conditions to the same population; stability or trustworthiness of a test.

Semantic classes. Associations between related words and concepts.

Semantic implications. Cause-effect relationships.

Semantic relations. Logical relations between words and concepts.

Semantic systems. A group of words having similar meanings; often termed verbal systems.

Semantic transformations. Redefinitions of words and concepts.

Semantic units. Words and concepts.

Sound blending. Blending into complete word phonetic sounds given orally, e.g., "c-u-p" and "b-o-a-t."

Spatial relationships. Refers to ability to perceive relationships among symbols as well as to oneself.

Split-half reliability. An estimate of the internal consistency of reliability.

Tactile. Referring to sense of touch.

Task analysis. Direct assessment of academic and/or behavioral deficits plus remediation, but without specification of underlying cause.

Test-retest reliability. The relationships or correlation between scores from two administrations of the same test to the same individuals.

Uniovular twins. Twins from the same ovum, identical twins.

Validity. Referring to a testing instrument's ability to evaluate what it proposes to assess.

Verbal expression. Expressions of a variety of concepts about familiar object.

Visual association. Ability to make generalizations from visual symbols.

Visual closure. Ability to identify visual stimulus from incomplete representation, e.g., child identifies partially pictured dogs.

Visual-motor coordination. Ability to coordinate vision with various body movements.

Visual perception. World as it seems to be by evaluation of visual stimuli.

Visual reception. Ability to derive meaning from visual symbols.

Visual sequential memory. Ability to recall and reproduce a series of nonmeaningful symbols.

REFERENCES

Ackerman, P. T., Peters, J. E., and Dykman, R. A. Children with specific learning disabilities: WISC profiles. *Journal of Learning Disabilities,* 1971, *4*, 150-166.

Adelman, A. S. The not-so-specific learning disability population: I. An interaction view of the causes of learning problems. II. Identification and correction through sequential teaching strategies. *Academic Therapy,* 1970-1971, Winter, Vol. 6, 117-123.

Adkins, P. L., Holmes, G. R., and Schnackenber, R. C. Factor analysis of the de Hirsch predictive index. *Perceptual and Motor Skills,* 1971, *33,* 1319-1325.

Ahr, A. E. The development of a group preschool screening test of early school entrance potential. *Psychology in the Schools,* 1967, *4* (1), 59-63.

Ali, F., and Costello, J. Modification of the Peabody Picture Vocabulary Test. *Developmental Psychology,* 1971, July, *5* (1), 86-91.

American Psychological Association. *Standards for Educational and Psychological Tests.* Washington, D.C., 1966.

Ames, L. B. Children with perceptual problems may also lag developmentally. *Journal of Learning Disabilities,* 1969, *2,* 205-209.

·Amundson, M. S. A preliminary screening program to identify functioning strengths and weaknesses in preschool children. Thesis, Moor-
head State College, Minn., 1972.

Anasara, A. Sample performance on the Slingerland screening tests with
commentary. Cambridge, Mass.: Educators Publishing Service,
1968.

Ashlock, P., and Stephen, A. *Educational therapy in the elementary
school.* Springfield, Ill.: Charles C. Thomas, 1966.

Association for Children with Learning Disabilities. Annual conference.
Meeting of executives and selected professionals in New York.
Pittsburgh: ACLD Headquarters, 1967.

Aten, J. L. Auditory memory and auditory sequencing. *Acta Sym-
bolica,* 1974, *5,* 38-65.

Aten, J., and Davis, J. Disturbances in the perception of auditory
sequencing in children with minimal cerebral dysfunction.
Journal of Speech and Hearing Research, 1968, *11,* 236-245.

Atlus, G. F. A WISC profile for retarded readers. *Journal of Consulting
Psychology,* 1952, *16,* 155-156.

Attwell, A., Orpert, R., and Meyers, C. E. Kindergarten behavior ratings
as a predictor of academic achievement. *Journal of School
Psychology,* 1967, *6,* 43-46.

Bangs, T. E. *Vocabulary comprehension scale.* Austin, Tex.: Learning
Concepts, 1975.

Bannatyne, A. The etiology of dyslexia and the color phonics system.
Paper presented at the Third Annual Conference of the Association for Children with Learning Disabilities., Tulsa, Okla., March,
1966.

Bannatyne, A. Diagnosing learning disabilities and writing remedial prescriptions. *Journal of Learning Disabilities,* 1968, *1* (4), 28-35.

Bannatyne, A. *Language, reading and learning disabilities.* Springfield,
Ill.: Charles C. Thomas, 1971.

Barsch, R. A. *Learning disabilities: A statement of position.* Washington, D.C.: Association for Children with Learning Disabilities, 1967.

Bateman, B. Learning disabilities—yesterday, today, and tomorrow. *Exceptional Children,* 1964, *31,* 167-177.

Bateman, B. Learning disorders. *Review of Educational Research,* 1966, *36* (1), 93-119.

Baumeister, A. A., and Bartlett, C. J. A comparison of the factor structure of normals and retardates on the WISC. *American Journal of Mental Deficiency,* 1962, *71,* 641-646.

Becker, L. D. Predicting learning disabilities: A pilot investigation. Research Report, University of California, Los Angeles, 1971.

Beery, K. E., and Buktenica, N. A. *Beery-Buktenica developmental test of visual-motor integration.* Chicago: Follet, 1967.

Belmont, I., and Birch, H. G. The intellectual profile of retarded readers. *Perceptual and Motor Skills,* 1966, *22,* 787-816.

Bender, L. *A visual motor gestalt test and its clinical use.* New York: The American Orthopsychiatric Association, 1938.

Bender, L. Problems in conceptualizing and communication in children with developmental alexis. In P. H. Hoch and J. Zubin, eds., *Psychopathology of communication.* New York: Grune and Stratton, 1958.

Berko, M. The child's learning of English morphology. *Word,* 1958, *14,* 150-177.

Berkowitz, R., and Rothman, E. Remedial reading for the disturbed child. *Clearing House,* 1955, *30,* 165-168.

Bice, H. V., and Cruickshank, W. M. The evaluation of intelligence. In W. M. Cruickshank, ed., *Cerebral palsy: Its individual and community problems,* 2nd ed. Syracuse, N.Y.: Syracuse University Press, 1966.

Birch, H. G. The problem of "brain damage" in children. In H. G. Birch, ed., *Brain damage in children: The biological and social aspects.* Baltimore: William and Wilkins, 1964.

Birch, H. G., and Grotberg, E., eds. Designs and proposals for early childhood research: A new look: Malnutrition, learning and intelligence. Washington, D.C.: Office of Economic Opportunity, Office of Planning, Research, and Evaluation, 1971.

Board of Education, Union, New Jersey. A program for the identification and remediation of perceptual deficiencies in kindergarten and primary grade students. Washington, D.C.: U.S. Department of Health, Education, and Welfare, Office of Education, April, 1968.

Boise, L. M. Emotional and personality problems of a group of retarded readers. *Elementary English,* 1955, *32,* 544-548.

Bonaker, R. Survey and evaluation to determine the educational needs in Butler and Lawrence Counties. Final Report, Planning Grant OEG 1-6-661091-116616, Washington, D.C.: U.S. Department of Health, Education, and Welfare, Office of Education, 1967.

Bond, G., and Fay, L. D. Comparison of the performance of good and poor readers on the individual items of the Stanford-Binet Intelligence Scale items (Forms L & M). *Journal of Educational Research,* 1950, *43,* 475-479.

Bortner, M. Perceptual skills and early reading disability. In L. Mann and D. A. Sabatino, eds., *The second review of special education.* Philadelphia: Journal of Special Education Press, 1974.

Boshes, B., and Myklebust, H. R. A neurological and behavioral study of children with learning disorders. *Neurology,* 1964, *14* (1), 7-12.

Brain, R. *Speech disorders: Aphasia, apraxia, and agnosia.* Washington, D.C.: Butterworth, 1961.

Brown, R., and Bellugi, I. Three processes in the acquisition of syntax. *Harvard Educational Review,* 1964, *34,* 133-151.

Bruininks, R. H. Prevalence of learning disabilities: Findings, issues, and recommendations. Research Report No. 20. Minnesota University, Minneapolis. Research, Development, and Demonstration Center in Education of Handicapped Children. Washington, D.C.: Bureau of Education for Handicapped, U.S. Department of Health, Education, and Welfare, Office of Education, June, 1971.

Bryan, T. S., and McGrady, H. J. Use of a teacher rating scale. *Journal of Learning Disabilities,* 1972, *5,* 199-206.

Buktenica, N.A. Identification of learning disabilities. *Journal of Learning Disabilities,* 1971, *4* (7), 379-383.

Bullock, L., and Brown, R. Behavioral dimensions in emotionally disturbed children. *Exceptional Children,* 1972, *38,* 740-741.

Burks, H. F., and Bruce, P. Characteristics of poor and good readers as disclosed by the Wechsler Intelligence Scale for Children. *Journal of Educational Psychology,* 1955, *46,* 488-493.

Bush, W. J., and Giles, M. T. *Aids to psycholinguistic teaching.* Columbus, Ohio: Charles E. Merrill, 1969.

Carrow, E. The development of auditory comprehension of language structures in children. *Journal of Speech and Hearing Disorders,* 1968, *33,* 99-111.

Carrow, E. *Test for auditory comprehension of language.* Austin, Tex.: Urban Research Group, 1973.

Carrow, E. *Carrow elicited language inventory.* Austin, Tex.: Learning Concepts, 1974.

Chalfant, J. C., and Scheffelin, M. A. *Central processing dysfunctions in children.* Bethesda: National Institute of Neurological Diseases and Stroke, Monograph No. 9, 1969.

Chansky, N. M. Threat, anxiety, and reading behavior. *Journal of Educational Research,* 1958, *51,* 333-340.

Chissom, B. S., and Thomas, J. R. Comparison of factor structures for the Frostig Developmental Test of Visual Perception. *Perceptual and Motor Skills,* 1971, *33,* 1015-1019.

Chissom, B. S., Thomas, J. R., and Biasiott, J. Canonical validity of perceptual-motor skills for predicting an academic criterion. *Educational and Psychological Measurements,* 1972, *32,* 1095-1098.

Chorost, S. B.; Spivack, G.; and Levine, M. Bender-Gestalt rotations and EEG abnormalities in children. *Journal of Consulting Psychology,* Dec. 23, 1959, *4,* 559.

Clawson, A. The Bender Visual Motor-Gestalt Test as an index of emotional disturbances in children. *Journal of Projective Techniques,* 1959, *23,* 198-206.

139

Clawson, A. Relationship of psychological tests to cerebral disorders in children: A pilot study. *Psychological Reports,* 1962, *10* (1), 187-190.

Clements, S. D. *Minimal brain dysfunction in children.* Terminology and identification - Phase I, NINDB Monograph No. 3. Washington, D.C.: U.S. Department of Health, Education, and Welfare, 1966.

Cobb, J. Relationship of discrete classroom behaviors to fourth-grade academic achievement. *Journal of Educational Psychology,* 1972, *63,* 74-80.

Cohen, J. Factorial structure of the WISC at ages 7.6, 10.6, and 13.6. *Journal of Consulting Psychology,* 1959, *23,* 285-299.

Coleman, J. C., and Rasof, B. Intellectual factors in learning disabilities. *Perceptual and Motor Skills,* 1963, *16* (1), 139-152.

Connolly, C. The psychosocial adjustment of children with dyslexia. *Exceptional Children,* 1969, *36,* 126-127.

Connolly, C. Social and emotional factors in learning disabilities. In H. R. Myklebust, ed., *Progress in learning disabilities,* Vol. II. New York: Grune and Stratton, 1971.

Conrad, W. G., and Tobiessen, J. The development of kindergarten behavior rating scales for the prediction of learning behavior disorders. *Psychology in the Schools,* 1967, *4,* 359-363.

Council for Exceptional Children. Annual convention papers. Arlington, Va., 1967.

Council for Exceptional Children. Annual convention papers. Arlington, Va., 1971.

Coy, M. N. The Bender Visual-Motor Gestalt Test as a predictor of academic achievement. *Journal of Learning Disabilities,* 1974, *7,* 317-319.

Cundick, B. P. Measures of intelligence on southwest Indian students. *Journal of School Psychology,* 1970, *81,* 151-156.

de Hirsch, K., Jansky, J. J., and Langford, W. S. The prediction of reading, spelling, and writing disabilities in children: A preliminary study. Final report to the Health Research Council of the City of New York, Contract U-1270. New York: Columbia

University, 1965.

de Hirsch, K., Jansky, J. J., and Langford, W. S. *Predicting reading failure: A preliminary study.* New York: Harper and Row, 1966.

Delacato, C. H. *The treatment and prevention of reading problems.* Springfield, Ill.: Charles C. Thomas, 1959.

Delacato, C. H. *The diagnosis and treatment of speech and reading problems.* Springfield, Ill.: Charles C. Thomas, 1963.

Denhoff, E., Hainsworth, P., and Hainsworth, M. Learning disabilities and early childhood education: An information-processing approach. In H. R. Myklebust, ed., *Progress in learning disabilities,* Vol. II, pp. 111-150. New York: Grune and Stratton, 1971.

Denhoff, E., Siqueland, M., Komich, M., and Hainsworth, P. Developmental and predictive characteristics of items from the Meeting Street Screening Test. *Developmental Medicine and Child Neurology,* 1967, *10,* 220-232.

Doehring, D. G. Visual spatial memory in aphasic children. *Journal of Speech and Hearing Research,* 1960, *3,* 242-249.

Dudek, S. A., and Lester, E. P. The good child facade in chronic underachievers. *American Journal of Orthopsychiatry,* 1968, *38,* 153-160.

Dunn, L. M. *Peabody picture vocabulary test.* Minneapolis: American Guidance Service, 1959.

Durost, W. N., Bixler, H. H., and Hildreth, G. H. *Metropolitan achievement tests and manual for interpreting.* Chicago: World Books Co., 1959.

Durost, W. N., Bixler, H. H., Wrightstone, J. W., Prescot, G. A., and Balow, I. H. *Metropolitan achievement tests.* New York: Harcourt, Brace and World, 1958.

Durrell, D. D. *Durrell analysis of reading difficulty.* New York: Harcourt, Brace and World, 1955.

Dykman, R. A., Ackerman, P. T., Clements, S. D., and Peters, J. E. Specific learning disabilities: An additional deficit syndrome. In H. R. Myklebust, ed., *Progress in learning disabilities,* Vol. II. New York: Grune and Stratton, 1971.

Eaves, L. C., Kendall, D. C., and Crichton, J. U. The early detection of minimal brain dysfunction. *Journal of Learning Disabilities,* 1972, *5,* 454-462.

Engleman, S. *Basic concepts inventory.* Chicago: Follett Educational Corporation, 1967.

Fargo, G., Roth, C., and Cade, T. Evaluation of an inter-disciplinary approach to prevention of early school failure. Technical Report, University of Hawaii, Honolulu, 1968.

Farrald, R. R., and Schamber, R. G. *Handbook I: A mainstream approach to identification, assessment and amelioration of learning disabilities.* Sioux Falls, S. Dak.: ADAPT Press, 1973.

Faust, M. Cognitive and language factors. In B. K. Keogh, ed., Early identification of children with potential learning problems. *Journal of Special Education,* 1970, *4,* 335-346.

Fisher, S. Learning disabilities in children. Sibling studies: Two sets of perceptual-motor function: The Draw-A-Person and the Bender-Gestalt. *Bulletin of the Orton Society,* 1968, *18,* 55-61.

Forness, S. R. Classroom observation of potential special education children. Technical Report, University of California, Los Angeles, 1972.

Foster, C. R.; Giddan, J. J.; and Stark, J. *ACLC: Assessment of children's language comprehension.* Palo Alto, Calif.: Consulting Psychologists Press, 1972.

Frantz, R. S. Ontogeny of perception. In A. M. Schrier, H. E. Harlow, and F. Stollnitz, eds., *Behavior of non-human primates: Modern research trends,* Vol. II. New York: Academic Press, 1965.

Frantz, R. S. Pattern discrimination and selective attention as determinants of perceptual development from birth. In A. Kidd and J. Rivoire, eds., *Perceptual development in children.* New York: International Universities, 1966.

Freeman, R. D. Special education and the electroencephalogram: Marriage of convenience. *The Journal of Special Education,* 1967, *2* (1), 61-73.

Frostig, M. *Developmental test of visual perception.* Palo Alto, Calif.: Consulting Psychologists Press, 1964.

Frostig, M. In J. M. Kauffman and D. P. Hallahan, eds., *Teaching chil-*

dren with learning disabilities: Personal perspectives. Columbus, Ohio: Charles E. Merrill, 1976.

Frostig, M., Lefever, W., and Whittlesey, J. Disturbance in visual perception. *Journal of Educational Research,* 1963, *33.* 665-671.

Frostig, M., and Maslow, P. *Learning problems in the classroom.* New York: Grune and Stratton, 1973.

Fuller, G. B. Introduction of a new orientation for Wertheimer's gestalt figures to be called the Minnesota Percepto-Diagnostic Test. Phase I — Children. Paper read at Minnesota Psychological Association Meeting, 1962.

Fuller, G. B., and Laird, J. T. The Minnesota Percepto-Diagnostic Test. *Journal of Clinical Psychology, 19,* Monograph Supplement No. 16, 1963.

Gallagher, J. A comparison of brain injured and non-brain injured mentally retarded children on several psychological variables. *Monographs of the Society for Research in Child Development,* 1957, *22,* 3-79.

Gallagher, J. J. Educational methods for brain-damaged children. In J. H. Masserman, ed., *Current psychiatric therapies.* New York: Grune and Stratton, 1962.

Gallagher, J. J. Children with developmental imbalances: A psycho-educational definition. In W. M. Cruickshank, ed., *The teacher of brain-injured children.* Syracuse, N.Y.: Syracuse University Press, 1966.

Gates, A. I. The Gates primary reading tests. *Teachers College Record,* 1926, *28,* 146-178.

Gates, A. I. *Gates reading readiness test.* New York: Teachers College Press, 1939.

Gates, A. I., and MacGinitie, W. H. *Gates-MacGinitie reading test.* New York: Teachers College Press, 1972.

Gates, A. I., and McKillop, A. S. *Gates-McKillop reading diagnostic tests.* New York: Teachers College Press, 1962.

Gellhorn, E., and Loofborrow, G. N. *Emotions and emotional behavior.* New York: Hoeber, 1963.

Goldberg, L. R. The effectiveness of clinicians' judgments: The diagnosis of organic brain damage from the Bender-gestalt test.

143

Journal of Consulting Psychology, 1959, *23,* 25-33.

Goldman, R., and Fristoe, M. *Goldman-Fristoe test of articulation.* Circle Pines, Minn.: American Guidance Service, 1969.

Goldman, R.; Fristoe, M.; and Woodcock, R. *Goldman-Fristoe-Woodcock test of auditory discrimination.* Circle Pines, Minn.: American Guidance Service, 1970.

Goldstein, S. A study of the self concepts of selected boys with learning disabilities. Unpublished master's thesis, University of Kansas, 1970.

Goodenough, F. L. *Measurement of intelligence by drawings.* Yonkers-on-Hudson, N.Y.: World Book Co., 1926.

Goodglass, H., and Kaplan, E. *The assessment of aphasia and related disorders.* Philadelphia: Lea and Febiger, 1972.

Graham, E. F. Wechsler-Bellevue and WISC scattergrams of unsuccessful readers. *Journal of Consulting Psychology,* 1952, *16,* 268-271.

Graham, F. K., and Kendall, D. C. *Memory-for-designs test—revised general manual.* Missoula, Mont.: Psychological Test Specialists, 1960.

Grenn, O. C.. and Perlman, S. M. Endocrinology and disorders of learning. In H. R. Myklebust, ed., *Progress in learning disabilities,* Vol. II. New York: Grune and Stratton, 1971.

Griffith, R. M., and Taylor, V. H. Incidence of Bender-gestalt figure rotations. *Journal of Consulting Psychology,* 1960, *24,* 189-190.

Griffiths, A. D., and Griffiths, P. W. Learning disabilities: Etiology. *Optometric Weekly,* 1974, *65,* 928-932.

Hainsworth, P., and Siqueland, M. *Early identification of children with learning disabilities: The Meeting Street School Screening Test.* Providence, R.I.: Crippled Children and Adults of Rhode Island, 1969.

Hallahan, D. P., and Kauffman, J. M. *Introduction to learning disabilities: A psycho-behavioral approach.* Englewood Cliffs, N.J.: Prentice-Hall, 1976.

Hammill, D. D. Evaluating children for instructional purposes. *Academic Therapy,* 1971, *1* (4), 341-353.

Hammill, D. D. Assessing and training perceptual-motor processes. In D. D. Hammill and N. R. Bartel, eds., *Teaching children with learning and behavior problems.* Boston: Allyn and Bacon, 1975.

Hammill, D. D., and Bartel, N. R., eds., *Teaching children with learning and behavior problems.* Boston: Allyn and Bacon, 1975.

Haring, N. G., and Bateman, B. D. *Minimal brain dysfunction in children: Educational, medical and health related services. - Phase II,* NTSDCP Monograph. Washington, D.C.: U.S. Department of Health, Education, and Welfare, 1969.

Haring, N. G., and Ridgway, R. W. Early identification of children with learning disabilities. *Exceptional Children,* Feb. 1967, 387-395.

Harris, A. J. *Harris test of lateral dominance.* New York: Psychological Corporation, 1947.

Harris, A. J. *How to increase reading ability,* 4th ed. New York: Longman's Green, 1961.

Harris, D. B. *Children's drawings as a measure of intellectual maturity: A revision of the Goodenough-Harris Draw-A-Man Test.* New York: Harcourt, Brace and World, 1963.

Havnik, L. J. A note on the limitations of the use of the Bender-gestalt as a diagnostic aid in patients with a functional complaint. *Journal of Clinical Psychology,* 1951, *7,* 194.

Havnik, L. J. A note on rotations in the Bender-gestalt tests as predictors of EEG abnormalities in children. *Journal of Clinical Psychology,* 1953, *9,* 399.

Hebb, D. O. The mammal and his environment. *American Journal of Psychiatry,* 1958, *41,* 826-831.

Henig, M. S. Predictive value of a reading readiness test and of teachers' forecasts. *Elementary School Journal,* 1949, *50,* 41-46.

Hermann, R. K. Congenital word-blindness (Poor readers in the light of Gerstmann's Syndrome). *Acta Psychiatrica et Neurologica Scandinavica Supplement,* 1956, *108,* 177-184.

Hermann, R. K. *Reading disability: A neurological study of reading disability and of related language disorders.* Springfield, Ill.: Charles C. Thomas, 1959.

Himelstein, P. Review of the Slosson Intelligence Test. In O. K. Buros, ed., *The seventh mental measurements yearbook*. Highland Park, N.J.: Gryphon Press, 1972.

Hinshelwood, J. *Congenital word-blindness*. London: H. K. Lewis, 1917.

Hirshorn, A. Comparison of the predictive validity of the revised Stanford-Binet Intelligence Scale and the Illinois Test of Psycholinguistic Abilities. *Exceptional Children*, 1969, *35*, 517-521.

Hirst, L. C. The usefulness of a two way analysis of WISC sub-tests in the diagnosis of remedial reading problems. *Journal of Experimental Education*, 1960, *29*, 155-156.

Hoffman, M. S. Early identification of learning problems. *Academic Therapy*, 1971, *7*, 23-35.

Horst, M. Het Onderzook van de Leesrijpheid by Zesjarige Kinderen. *Nederlands Tijdschrift voor de psychologie*, 1958, *13*.

Hunt, J. V. Review of the Slosson Intelligence Test. In O. K. Buros, ed., *The seventh mental measurements yearbook*. Highland Park, N.J.: Gryphon Press, 1972.

Ilg, F. L., and Ames, R. B. *School readiness: Behavior tests used at the Gesell Institute*. New York: Harper and Row, 1964.

Ilg, F., Ames, L. B., and Appel, R. J. School readiness as evaluated by Gessel Development, Visual and Predictive Tests. *Genetic Psychology Monographs*, 1965, *71*, 61-91.

Jamison, C. B. Review of the Purdue Perceptual-Motor Survey. In O. K. Buros, ed., *The seventh mental measurements yearbook*. Highland Park, N. J.: Gryphon Press, 1972.

Jastak, J. F., and Jastak, S. R. *Wide range achievement test*. Los Angeles: Western Psychological Services, 1965.

Jenkins, N., Spivack, G., Levine, M., and Savage, W. Wechsler profiles and academic achievement in emotionally disturbed boys. *Journal of Consulting Psychology*, 1964, *28*, 290.

Jens, D. Project Genesis. Final Report. Lakeshore Public Schools, St. Clair Shores, Mich., Bureau of Elementary and Secondary Information. Washington, D.C.: U. S. Department of Health, Education, and Welfare, Office of Education, 1970.

146

Johnson, D. J. Treatment approaches to dyslexia. *International Reading Association: Conference Proceedings,* 1969, *13,* 95-102.

Johnson, D. J., and Myklebust, H. R. *Learning disabilities: Educational principles and practices.* New York: Grune and Stratton, 1967.

Johnson, S. W., and Morasky, R. L. *Learning disabilities.* Boston: Allyn and Bacon, 1977.

Kallos, C. L., Grabow, J. M., and Guarine, E. A. The WISC profile of disabled readers. *Personnel and Guidance Journal,* 1961, *39,* 467-478.

Karlsen, B., Madden, R., and Gardner, E. F. *Stanford diagnostic reading test.* New York: Harcourt Brace Jovanovich, 1966.

Kass, C. E. Some psychological correlates of severe reading disability (dyslexia). *Selected studies on the Illinois Test of Psycholinguistic Abilities.* Madison, Wis.: Xer-Lith Service, Photo Press, 1963, 87-96.

Kelley, T. L.; Madden, R.; Gardner, E. F.; and Rudman, H. C. *Stanford achievement test.* New York: Harcourt, Brace and World, 1964.

Keogh, B. K. The Bender gestalt as a predictive diagnostic test of reading performance. *Journal of Consulting Psychology,* 1965, *29,* 83-84.

Keogh, B. K. The Bender-gestalt with children: Research implications. *Journal of Special Education,* 1969, *3,* 15-22.

Keogh, B. K., and Becker, L. D. Early detection of learning problems: Questions, cautions, and guidelines. *Exceptional Children,* 1973, *40* (1), 5-11.

Keogh, B., and Smith, C. E. Group techniques and proposed scoring system for the Bender-gestalt test with children. *Journal of Clinical Psychology,* 1961, *17,* 172-175.

Keogh, B., and Smith, C. E. Visuo-motor ability for school prediction: A seven year study. *Perceptual and Motor Skills,* 1967, *25,* 101-110.

Keogh, B. K., and Smith, C. E. Early identification of educationally high potential and high risk children. *Journal of School Psychology,* 1970, *8,* 285-290.

Keogh, B. K., and Tchir, C. Teachers' perceptions of educationally high risk children. Technical Report, University of California, Los Angeles, 1972.

Keogh, B. K., Wetter, J., McGinty, A., and Donlon, G. Functional analysis of WISC performance of learning disorders, hyperactive, and mentally retarded boys. *Psychology in the Schools,* 1973, *10,* 178-181.

Kephart, N. C. *The slow learner in the classroom.* Columbus, Ohio: Charles E. Merrill, 1960, 1971.

Kephart, N. C. Review of Frostig Developmental Test of Visual Perception. In O. K. Buros, ed., *The seventh mental measurements yearbook.* Highland Park, N.J.: Gryphon Press, 1972.

Kephart, N. C. Perceptual-motor problems of children. In S. A. Kirk and J. M. McCarthy, eds., *Learning disabilities: Selected ACLD papers.* Boston: Houghton Mifflin, 1975.

Kirk, S. A. *Educating exceptional children.* Boston: Houghton Mifflin, 1967.

Kirk, S. A. Illinois Test of Psycholinguistic Abilities: Its origins and implications. In J. Hellmuth, ed., *Learning disorders,* Vol. 3. Seattle: Special Child Publications, 1968.

Kirk, S. A. Behavioral diagnosis and remediation of learning disabilities. In S. A. Kirk and J. M. McCarthy, eds., *Learning disabilities: Selected ACLD papers.* Boston: Houghton Mifflin, 1975.

Kirk, S. A. In J. M. Kauffman and D. P. Hallahan, eds., *Teaching children with learning disabilities: Personal perspectives.* Columbus, Ohio: Charles E. Merrill, 1976.

Kirk, S. A., and McCarthy, J. J. *The Illinois Test of Psycholinguistic Abilities,* rev. ed. Urbana, Ill.: University of Illinois Press, 1968.

Kleffner, F. F. Aphasia and other language deficiencies in children: Research and teaching at Central Institute for the Deaf. In W. T. Daley, ed., *Speech and language therapy with the brain-damaged child.* Washington, D.C.: Catholic University of America Press, 1962.

Kling, M. In O. K. Buros, ed., *The seventh mental measurements yearbook.* Highland Park, N.J.: The Gryphon Press, 1972.

Koenigsknecht, R. In L. L. Lee, *Developmental sentence scoring.* Evanston, Ill.: Northwestern University Press, 1974.

Koppitz, E. M. The Bender-gestalt and learning disturbances in young children. *Journal of Clinical Psychology,* 1958, *14,* 292-295.

Koppitz, E. M. *The Bender-gestalt test for young children.* New York: Grune and Stratton, 1964.

Laird, J. T. Differentiating adult brain-damaged from normals and emotionally disturbed by use of the Minnesota Percepto-Diagnostic Test. Paper read at Minnesota Psychological Association Meeting, 1962.

Learner, J. N. *Children with learning disabilities.* Boston: Houghton Mifflin, 1976.

Lee, L. L. *Developmental sentence scoring.* Evanston, Ill.: Northwestern University Press, 1974.

Lovitt, T. C. Assessment of children with learning disabilities. In R. H. Bradford, ed., *Behavior modification of learning disabilities.* San Rafael, Calif.: Academic Therapy Publications, 1971.

Luria, A. The role of speech in the regulation of normal and abnormal behavior. In J. Tizard, ed., *The mentally handicapped and their families.* New York: Liveright, 1961.

Lyle, J. G., and Goyen, J. Performance of retarded readers on the WISC and educational tests. *Journal of Abnormal Psychology,* 1969, *74,* 105-112.

Lyman, H. H. Review of the Peabody Picture Vocabulary Test. In O. K. Buros, ed., *The sixth mental measurements yearbook.* Highland Park, N.J.: Gryphon Press, 1965.

McCarthy, J. J. Selected convention papers. Council for Exceptional Children. Denver, Colo., April, 1969.

McCarthy, J. J., and McCarthy, J. F. *Learning disabilities.* Boston: Allyn and Bacon, 1969.

McCarthy, J. M. In J. M. Kauffman and D. P. Hallahan, eds., *Teaching children with learning disabilities: Personal perspectives.* Columbus, Ohio: Charles E. Merrill, 1976.

McDonald, C. W. Problems concerning the classification and education

149

of children with learning disabilities. In J. Hellmuth, ed., *Learning disabilities,* Vol. 3. Seattle: Special Child Publications, 1968.

McGrady, H. J. Learning disabilities: Implications for medicine and education. Paper presented at ASHA-AMA Pre-Convention Session on School Health, Chicago, June, 1970.

McLeod, J. Prediction of childhood dyslexia. *The Slow Learning Child,* 1966, *12,* 143-155.

Magoon, J., and Cox, R. C. An evaluation of the Screening Test for Academic Readiness. *Educational and Psychological Measurement,* 1969, *29* (4), 941-950.

Mardell, C. A., and Goldenberg, D. S. Learning disability/early childhood research project. Annual Report. Springfield, Ill.: Illinois State Office of the Superintendent of Public Instruction, Aug., 1972.

Meier, J. H. Prevalence and characteristics of learning disabilities found in second grade children. *Journal of Learning Disabilities,* 1971, *4,* 1-16.

Miller, C. K., Chansky, N. M., and Gredler, G. R. Rater agreement on WISC protocols. *Psychology in the Schools,* 1970, *7,* 190-193.

Minskoff, E., Wiseman, D. C., and Minskoff, J. G. *The MWM program for developing language abilities.* Ridgefield, N.J.: Educational Performance Associates, 1972.

Money, J., ed. *Reading disability: Progress in research needs in dyslexia.* Baltimore: Johns Hopkins Press, 1962.

Monroe, M. *Children who cannot read.* Chicago: University of Chicago Press, 1932.

Myers, P. I., and Hammill, D. D. *Methods for learning disorders.* New York: John Wiley and Sons, 1969.

Myklebust, H. *Auditory disorders in children: A manual for differential diagnosis.* New York: Grune and Stratton, 1954.

Myklebust, H. R. *Picture story language test.* New York: Grune and Stratton, 1965.

Myklebust, H. R. *Progress in learning disabilities, Volume I.* New York: Grune and Stratton, 1968.

Myklebust, H. R. What do we mean by learning disorders? In S. A. Kirk and J. M. McCarthy, eds., *Learning disabilities: Selected ACLD papers.* Boston: Houghton Mifflin, 1975.

Myklebust, H. R., and Boshes, B. Minimal brain damage in children. Final Report U.S.P.H.S. Contract 108-65-142. Washington, D.C.: U.S. Department of Health, Education, and Welfare, 1969.

Neville, D. A comparison of the WISC patterns of male retarded and non-retarded readers. *Journal of Educational Research,* 1961, *54,* 195-197.

Neville, D., and Bruininks, R. H. Reading and intelligence. In H. C. Haywood, ed., *Psychometric intelligence.* New York: Appleton-Century-Crofts, 1972.

Newcomer, P. L., and Hammill, D. D. *Psycholinguistics in the schools.* Columbus, Ohio: Charles E. Merrill, 1976.

Northwestern University. Northwestern syntax screening test (NSST). Evanston, Ill.: Northwestern University Press, 1969.

Novack, H. S., Bonaventura, E., and Merenda, P. F. A scale for early detection of children with learning problems. *Exceptional Children,* 1973, *40,* 98-105.

Orton, S. T. Specific reading disability - Strephosymbolia. *Journal of the American Medical Association,* 1928 (April), *90,* 1095-1099.

Osborne, R. T., and Tillman, M. H. Normal and retarded WISC performances. *American Journal of Mental Deficiency,* 1967, *72,* 257-261.

Osgood, C. E. *Method and theory in experimental psychology.* New York: Oxford University Press, 1953.

Otis, A. S. *Otis quick-scoring mental ability test.* New York: Harcourt Brace Jovanovich, 1954.

Ozer, M. N., and Richardson, H. B. Diagnostic evaluation of children with learning problems: A communication process. *Childhood Education,* 1972, *48,* 244-247.

Pate, J. E., and Webb, W. W. *First grade screening test.* Circle Pines, Minn.: American Guidance Service, 1966.

151

Penfield, W., and Roberts, L. *Speech and brain-mechanism.* New York: Princeton University Press, 1959.

Piers, E. V. Review of the Peabody Picture Vocabulary Test. In O. K. Buros, ed., *The sixth mental measurements yearbook.* Highland Park, N.J.: Gryphon Press, 1965.

Plantz, C. A. Report of a pilot program for identifying and remediating kindergarten children with potential learning problems. *Illinois School Research,* 1972, *9* (1), 18-22.

Popham, W. J., and Baker, E. D. *Systematic instruction.* Englewood Cliffs, N.J.: Prentice-Hall, 1970.

Porch, B. *Porch index of communicative ability in children.* Palo Alto, Calif.: Consulting Psychologists Press, 1974.

Proger, B. B. Pupil rating scale screening for learning disabilities. *Journal of Special Education,* 1973, *7,* 311-317.

Pronovost, W., and Dumbleton, C. A picture-type speech sound discrimination test. *Journal of Speech and Hearing Disorders,* 1953, *18,* 258-266.

Quay, H. C. Special education: Assumptions, techniques, and evaluative criteria. *Exceptional Children,* 1973, *40,* 165-170.

Rabinovitch, R. D. Reading and learning disabilities. In S. Arieti, ed., *American handbook of psychiatry,* Vol. 1. New York: Basic Books, 1959.

Rabinovitch, R. D. Educational achievement in children with psychiatric problems. *Bulletin of the Orton Society,* 1964, *14,* 1-5.

Rabinovitch, R. D., and Ingram, W. Neuropsychiatric considerations in reading retardation. *Reading Teacher,* 1962, *15,* 433-438.

Ransom, G. A. Review of First Grade Screening Test. *Journal of Educational Measurement,* 1969, *6* (1), 36-37.

Rappaport, S. R. Personality factors teachers need for relationship structure. In W. M. Cruickshank, ed., *The teacher of brain injured children.* Syracuse, N.Y.: Syracuse University Press, 1966.

Raskin, L. M., and Taylor, W. J. Problem identification through observation. *Academic Therapy,* 1973, *9,* 85-89.

Raven, J. C. *Progressive matrices.* London: H. K. Lewis and Co., Ltd., 1965.

Rees, N. S. Auditory processing factors in language disorders: The view from Procrustes' bed. *Journal of Speech and Hearing Disorders,* 1973, *38,* 304-315.

Reid, W. R., and Schoer, L. A. Reading achievement, social class, and subtest pattern of the WISC. *Journal of Educational Research,* 1966, *59,* 469-472.

Roach, E. G., and Kephart, N. C. *The Purdue perceptual-motor survey.* Columbus, Ohio: Charles E. Merrill, 1966.

Robeck, M. Intellectual strengths and weaknesses shown by reading clinic subjects on the WISC. *Journal of Educational Research,* 1964, *51,* 459-464.

Robinson, H. M. *Why pupils fail in reading.* Chicago: University of Chicago Press, 1946.

Robinson, H. M., and Gray, A. I. *Gray oral reading test.* Indianapolis, Ind.: Bobbs-Merrill, 1963.

Rocky Mountain Educational Laboratory. *Individual learning disabilities program: Pilot incidence study.* Vol. I, II, III. Greeley, Colo., 1969.

Rogolsky, M. M. Screening kindergarten children: A review and recommendation. *Journal of School Psychology,* 1968-1969, *7* (2), 18-27.

Rose, F. C. The occurrence of short auditory memory span among school children referred for diagnosis of reading difficulties. *Journal of Educational Research,* 1958, *51,* 459-464.

Rosenthal, R., and Jacobson, L. Teacher's expectancies as determinants of pupils' IQ gains. *Psychological Reports,* 1966, *19* (1), 115-118.

Rosner, J. *Helping children overcome learning disabilities.* New York: Walker and Co., 1975.

Rugel, R. P. WISC subtest scores of disabled readers: A review with respect to Bannatyne's recategorization. *Journal of Learning Disabilities,* 1974, *7* (1), 43-55.

Ryckman, D. B., and Rentfrow, R. K. The Beery Developmental Test of Visual-Motor Integration: An investigation of reliability. *Jour-*

nal of Learning Disabilities, 1971, *4* (6), 333-335.

Sapir, S., and Wilson, B. A developmental scale to assist in the prevention of learning disability. *Educational and Psychological Measurement,* 1967, *27,* 1061-1068.

Sattler, J. M. *Assessment of children's intelligence.* Philadelphia: W. B. Saunders, 1974.

Semel, E. M., and Wiig, E. H. Comprehension of syntactic structures and critical verbal elements by children with learning disabilities. *Journal of Learning Disabilities,* 1975, *8,* 53-58.

Senf, G., and Freundl, P. Memory and attention factors in specific learning disabilities. *Journal of Learning Disabilities,* 1971, *4,* 94-106.

Shriner, T. H., and Danieloff, R. G. Reassembly of segmented cvc syllables by children. *Journal of Speech and Hearing Research,* 1970, *13,* 537-547.

Silver, L. B. Familial patterns in children with neurologically based learning disabilities. *Journal of Learning Disabilities,* 1971, *4* (7), 349-358.

Simmons, G. A., and Shapiro, B. J. Reading expectancy formulas: A warning note. *Journal of Reading,* 1968, *11,* 626-629.

Skinner, B. F. *The technology of teaching.* New York: Appleton-Century-Crofts, 1968.

Skokie School District No. 68. A demonstration of technique in the identification, diagnosis, and treatment of children with learning disabilities. Skokie, Illinois. Washington, D.C.: U. S. Department of Health, Education, and Welfare, Office of Education, Bureau of Research, September, 1969.

Slingerland, B. H. *Screening tests for identifying children with specific language disability.* Cambridge, Mass.: Educators Publishing Service, 1962.

Slingerland, B. H. Public school programs for the prevention of specific language disability in children. In J. Hellmuth, ed., *Education therapy.* Seattle: Special Child Publications, 1966.

Sloan, W. *Lincoln-Osertsky motor development scale.* Los Angeles: Western Psychological Services, 1954.

Slosson, R. L. Slosson intelligence test (SIT) for children and adults. East Aurora, N.Y.: Slosson Educational Publications, 1963.

Smith, P. A., and Marx, R. W. Some cautions on the use of the Frostig test: A factor analytic study. *Journal of Learning Disabilities*, 1972, *5* (6), 357-362.

Snow, P. Unfinished pygmalion. *Contemporary Psychology*, 1969, *14*, 197-199.

Spivack, G., and Swift, M. *Devereux elementary school behavior rating scale manual.* Devon, Pa.: Devereux Foundation Press, 1967.

Spivack, G., Swift, M., and Prewitt, J. Syndromes of disturbed classroom behavior: A behavioral diagnostic system for elementary schools. *Journal of Special Education,* 1971, *5,* 269-292.

Stephens, T. M. *Teaching skills to children with learning and behavioral disorders.* Columbus, Ohio: Charles E. Merrill, 1977.

Strauss, A., and Lehtinen, L. *Psychopathology and education of the brain injured child.* New York: Grune and Stratton, 1947, 1971.

Tamkin, A. S. Survey of educational disability in emotionally disturbed children. *Journal of Educational Research,* 1960, *54,* 67-69.

Templin, M. *Certain language skills in children.* Minneapolis: University of Minnesota Press, 1957.

Templin, M. C., and Darley, F. L. *The Templin-Darley tests of articulation,* 2nd ed. Iowa City: University of Iowa, Bureau of Educational Research and Service, Extension Division, 1960.

Terman, L. M., and Merrill, M. A. *Stanford-Binet intelligence scale,* 3rd rev. Boston: Houghton Mifflin, 1960a.

Terman, L. M., and Merrill, M. A. *The Stanford-Binet intelligence scale: Manual for 3rd rev., Form L-M.* Boston: Houghton Mifflin, 1960b.

Thorndike, R. L. Review of pygmalion in the classroom by R. Rosenthal and L. Jacobson. *American Educational Research Journal,* 1968, *5,* 708-711.

Tiegs, E. W., and Clark, W. W. *California achievement tests.* New York: McGraw-Hill, 1957.

Tiegs, E. W., and Clark, W. W. *California achievement tests.* Monterey,

155

Calif.: California Test Bureau, 1970.

Tobiessen, J. , Duckworth, B., and Conrad, G. Relationships between the Schenectady Kindergarten Rating Scales and first grade achievement and adjustment. *Psychology in the Schools*, 1971, *8*, 29-96.

Trabasso, T. Pay attention. *Psychology Today*, 1968, *2*, 30-36.

Ullman, C. A. Prevalence of reading disabilities as a function of the measurement used. *Journal of Learning Disabilities*, 1969, (11), 626-629.

Wechsler, D. *Manual for the Wechsler intelligence scale for children*. New York: Psychological Corporation, 1949a.

Wechsler, D. *Wechsler intelligence scale for children*. New York: Psychological Corporation, 1949b, 1955.

Wedell, K. Perceptual-motor factors. In B. K. Keogh, ed., Early identification of children with potential learning problems. *Journal of Special Education* (Monograph Issue), 1970, *4*, 323-331.

Weener, P. S. Auditory discrimination and articulation. *Journal of Speech and Hearing Disorders*, 1967, *32*, 19-28.

Weener, P., Barnitt, M., and Melvyn, S. A critical evaluation of the Illinois Test of Psycholinguistic Abilities. *Exceptional Children*, 1967, *33*, 373-384.

Wepman, J. *Wepman auditory discrimination test*. Chicago: Chicago Language Research Associates, 1958.

Werry, J., Weiss, C., and Douglas, V. Studies on the hypoactive child: I. Some preliminary findings. *Canadian Psychiatric Association Journal*, 1964, *9*. 120-130.

Westman, J., Rice, D., and Bermann, E. Nursery school behavior and later school adjustment. *American Journal of Orthopsychiatry*, 1967, *37*, 725-732.

Whitsell, L. J. Neurological aspects of reading disorders. In R. M. Flower, H. F. Gofman, and L. Lawson, eds., *Reading disorders*. Philadelphia: F. A. Davis, 1965.

Wickman, E. K. *Children's behavior and teachers' attitudes*. New York: Oxford University Press, 1928.

Wiig, E. H., and Semel, E. M. Comprehension of linguistic concepts requiring logical operations by learning disabled children. *Journal of Speech and Hearing Research,* 1973, *16,* 627-636.

Wiig, E. H., and Semel, E. M. Productive language abilities in learning disabled adolescents. *Journal of Learning Disabilities,* 1975, *8,* 578-586.

Wiig, E. H., and Semel, E. M. *Language disabilities in children and adults.* Columbus, Ohio: Charles E. Merrill, 1976.

Wilborn, B. L., and Smith, P. A. Early identification of children with learning problems: Learning problem indication index. *Academic Therapy,* 1971, *9,* 363-371.

Witkin, H. A., Dyk, R., Faterson, H., Goodenough, D., and Karp, S. *Psychological differentiation.* New York: Wiley and Sons, 1962.

Ysseldyke, J. E., and Salvia, J. Diagnostic-prescriptive teaching: Two models. *Exceptional Children,* 1974, *40,* 181-185.

Zach, L., and Kaufman, J. How adequate is the concept of perceptual deficit for education? *Journal of Learning Disabilities,* 1972, *5* (6), 351-355.

Zangwill, O. *Cerebral dominance and its relation to psychological function.* Edinburgh: Oliver and Boyd, 1960.

Zeaman, D., and House, B. The role of attention in discrimination learning. In H. N. Ellis, ed., *Handbook of mental deficiency.* New York: McGraw-Hill, 1963.

AUTHOR INDEX

159

160

SUBJECT INDEX

167

About the Author

E. LaMonte Ohlson is senior faculty member at the Case Western Reserve University, Department of Psychiatry and Pediatrics and Director of the Learning Disabilities/Exceptional Children Clinic, Cleveland Metropolitan General Hospital, Cleveland, Ohio. He received his first doctorate degree in psychology from the University of Oklahoma and his second doctorate degree in statistics from American International University.

Dr. Ohlson has been the recipient of several grants for work in learning disabilities and has published extensively in the areas of learning disorders, human sexuality, and statistics.

171

Dr. Ohlson has held positions with private industry, government, and various universities. He also maintains a private clinical psychology practice and specializes in learning disorders, marital discord, and sexual dysfunctioning.